A Barna Report Produced
in Partnership with
Brotherhood Mutual

LEADERSHIP TRANSITIONS

How Churches
Navigate Pastoral
Change—and
Stay Healthy

Copyright © 2019 by Barna Group. All rights reserved.

ISBN: 978-1-945269-44-8

All information contained in this document is copyrighted by Barna Group and shall remain the property of Barna Group. U.S. and international copyright laws protect the contents of this document in their entirety. Any reproduction, modification, distribution, transmission, publication, translation, display, hosting or sale of all or any portion of the contents of this document is strictly prohibited without written permission of an authorized representative of Barna Group.

The information contained in this report is true and accurate to the best knowledge of the copyright holder. It is provided without warranty of any kind: express, implied or otherwise. In no event shall Barna Group or its respective officers or employees be liable for any special, incidental, indirect or consequential damages of any kind, or any damages whatsoever resulting from the use of this information, whether or not users have been advised of the possibility of damage, or on any theory of liability, arising out of or in connection with the use of this information.

Unless otherwise indicated, scripture quotations are from the *Holy Bible, New Living Translation* copyright ©1996, 2004, 2015 by Tyndale House Foundation. Used by permission of Tyndale House Publishers Inc., Carol Stream, Illinois 60188. All rights reserved.

Funding for this research was made possible by the generous support of Brotherhood Mutual. Barna Group was solely responsible for data collection, analysis and writing of the report.

Contents

Preface

by Mark A. Robison, Brotherhood Mutual 5

Introduction 9

1. **Before the Transition** 19

    Q&A with Bruce Terrell, Redeemer Church, New York City

    Q&A with Boz Tchividjian, GRACE

2. **During the Transition** 39

    Q&A with Mandy Smith, University Christian Church, Cincinnati, OH

    "The Dos & Don'ts of Communicating a Leadership Transition," by Samuel Ogles

3. **After the Transition** 67

    Q&A with Doug Sauder, Calvary Chapel, Fort Lauderdale, FL

    Q&A with Darrell Hall, Elizabeth Baptist Church, Conyers, GA

Conclusion

5 Marks of Successful Leadership Transition

by David Kinnaman 95

Appendix

A. Additional Contributors 103

B. Notes 105

C. Methodology 107

Acknowledgements 109

About the Project Partners 111

Preface

We are nearing a crucial juncture in church leadership. As the average age of pastors increases, there is growing concern about the need to identify and develop a new generation of leaders. In 1 Peter 5, God commands church leaders to shepherd his people. I believe a big part of shepherding is planning for the continuation of ministry after a pastor leaves the role. If your pastor stepped down from ministry today, how would your church respond?

Through this study, David Kinnaman and the team at Barna examine the pressing topic of leadership transition. While it's true that with every season there is change, change is difficult. It's often disruptive. Leadership change, in particular, represents a critical intersection of the old and new, the past and future which, while exciting for some, is unsettling for many. This research focuses on how pastors, church staff and congregations view the health of a church before, during and after leadership transition and highlights important issues to address during this pivotal time in the life of a ministry.

In our more than 100-year history, Brotherhood Mutual has experienced several leadership changes. I am privileged to follow four previous presidents. It's been humbling to continue the work of those who came before and to prepare the next generation to lead our company into the future. With each transition, we focused on communicating the vision and future of our company, while never losing sight of why we began.

Our mission is "Advancing the Kingdom by serving the Church." As we go about our daily work of insuring and protecting church buildings and ministry activities, our staff and independent agents see pastors struggling with the challenges of being a shepherd and leader. *Leadership Transitions* sheds important light on caring for outgoing and incoming pastors. It reminds us that pastors are human and provides us with opportunities to understand how local congregations can care for spiritual leaders and their families. The study also reveals that passing the baton from one generation to the next should be something pastors plan for as part of their ongoing ministry.

It's our prayer that this information will inspire current leaders to invest in future leaders and help congregations to care for their leaders. We hope this starts a conversation that ensures church leadership vitality now and until Christ's return.

Mark A. Robison
Chairman & President
Brotherhood Mutual Insurance Company

Leadership Transitions in Context

*B*arna analysts believe a shortage of pastors is on the horizon unless leaders and churches start now to identify, equip and release future church leaders. Here are three of the most significant factors that should put this issue on the front burner.

Aging Clergy

Half of all current senior pastors are over the age of 55. Twenty-five years ago—as young and middle adults—they made up three-quarters of all Protestant clergy. Twenty-five years from now, who will fill their shoes?

- 40 and under
- 41 to 55
- 56 to 64
- 65 and older

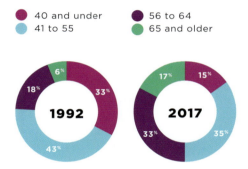

Shrinking Candidate Pool

Two out of three pastors say it's hard to identify future church leaders. Young Christians, many current pastors say, lack the necessary maturity or aren't interested in vocational ministry. Plus, only 14 percent of senior leaders rate themselves as "excellent" when it comes to mentoring younger leaders.

It is becoming harder to find mature young Christians who want to become pastors

A lot of young leaders seem to think other kinds of work are more important than vocational ministry

- agree strongly
- agree somewhat

Diminishing Cultural Credibility

Just one in five U.S. adults believes that pastors are a very credible source of insight on the most important issues of our day. It may become increasingly difficult to convince young leaders that pastoring a church is the best way to influence culture for the sake of God's kingdom.

- very credible
- somewhat credible
- not very credible
- not at all credible
- not sure

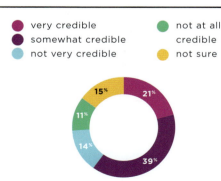

% among U.S. adults

Introduction

Barna often aims the lens of its research on topics that church leaders are concerned with today: the risk of burnout among senior pastors, churchgoers' views and habits related to evangelism, faith-sharing in the digital age, the logistics of adding a church campus, and so on. For the most part, these studies pertain to special interests or specific denominations, or perhaps highlight areas of outreach or growth that merit more attention and action from U.S. ministries. This particular report, however, based on a multifaceted study conducted in partnership with Brotherhood Mutual, is focused on an urgent reality that faces *all* ministries, whether or not they are actively considering it today: Someday, your current senior leader will no longer be there. As William Vanderbloemen and Warren Bird insist in *Next: Pastoral Succession That Works*, "Every pastor is an interim pastor."[1]

This inevitability—that no one will stay in a pulpit forever—eclipses other factors that differentiate ministry experiences, such as location, church size, primary ethnicity, denomination and so on. Whether because of retirement, scandal, health complications, a change in calling or some other shift in a pastor's life or career, every church will walk through a pastoral succession of some kind; most likely, multiple times.

This fact alone lends weight to the need for this research.

Beyond the necessity for individual churches to consider upcoming leadership transitions, the North American church as a whole is rapidly approaching a mass pastoral succession. In previous studies, Barna has examined the "graying" or aging of U.S. clergy; indeed, the median age of a Protestant senior pastor today is 54—up from age 44 in 1992. U.S. church leaders are primarily white male Boomers. What's more, the data indicates there has been some neglect in identifying, mentoring and raising up potential pastors for the future. Only one in seven pastors is under 40. This leaves driven, diverse younger generations—largely formed by the pressures of a secularizing society—untapped for ministry callings, or even unconvinced of these vocations' importance.

All things considered, pastoral succession is one of *the* most pressing issues in the Church today. How a church navigates a leadership transition impacts its ability to be effective on every other front: caring for those in need, providing theological instruction, confronting injustice, cultivating deep community, facilitating meaningful worship experiences and, ultimately, drawing people to know and follow Christ. An unsuccessful or messy pastoral succession process can compromise these mission-critical efforts. On the other hand, a positive process of transition can propel a church into a new season of fruitfulness.

IT'S TIME TO PASS THE BATON

"I was done. I had been there for 25 years, and the church needed new leadership. We needed fundamental, not just incremental, changes. The reality is that, when you lose momentum, there's virtually no example of the current pastor and his team being able to turn it around. I needed to get out of the way."

—Gary Kinnaman, former pastor of Hillsong, Phoenix, AZ

Barna designed a multi-pronged study to explore the process of leadership succession in U.S. Protestant churches, analyzing perspectives from the pulpit to the pew (incoming and outgoing pastors, as well as church staff and congregants) about each phase of a transition. While the conclusions of this study will be useful to churches in the midst of or looking back on a leadership change, they are best intended as insights for those anticipating and preparing for an upcoming pastoral succession.

If you or your church see a transition in your future, first of all, try not to worry. Yes, stakes are high, but under most circumstances—including abrupt and crisis transitions—a senior pastor's departure does *not* totally wreck a church. For nearly one-third of churches that undergo a leadership transition, the results are a clear gain. For most, outcomes are mixed, with only a small proportion experiencing negative results. And whatever a leadership team

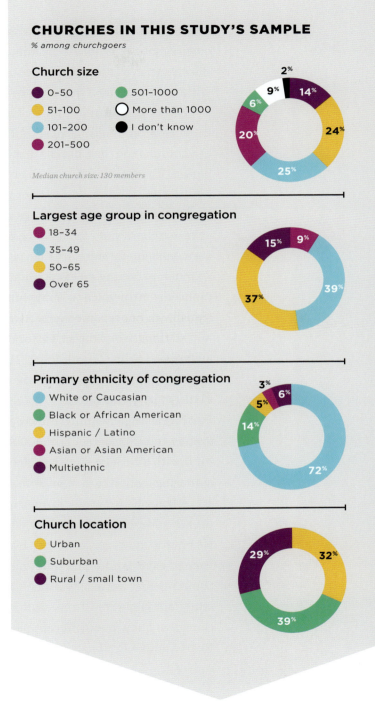

Introduction — 11

gets right or wrong about its succession approach, chances are the congregants are going to be okay; consistently, out of all four groups Barna surveyed about the process, churchgoers are the most buoyant witnesses to a leadership transition.

Although pastors and their teams are often reluctant to talk about it, succession should be an essential sign of the resilience and renewal of a church (and the Church) that is greater than any one personality or period. If you're thinking at all about the right agenda and method for a future succession, you are not wasting your time—any preparation at all appears to be an advantage to the eventual outcome. But, as other researchers and experts have found, Barna finds that "healthy succession is much more art than science."[2] As such, this report doesn't so much prescribe an exact plan as point to some powerful yet commonsense principles to guide and improve your church's leadership transition. The research reflects a wide range of church sizes, contexts and settings, which gives a broad base of insights for congregations of all types.

Analyzing the Data

Barna researchers mined the mountain of data gathered from the four groups (churchgoers, church staff, and incoming and outgoing pastors) with a variety of analytic tools. Two that proved most helpful for gathering insights are *regression* and *outcome segmentation.*

A church's progress through a transition is the result of a tangle of events and responses, each of which appears important in isolation. No church, however, is defined by just one feature or action. Churches vary in experiences and outcomes of a transition by many factors—sometimes, it seems, by all of them. Thus, many insights from this study are generated from regression analysis—basically, long equations that show how different pieces of data interact with each other. Regressions allow analysts to untangle the many factors of a transition and look at multiple variables at the same time, better answering questions such as:

- What factors of a transition are important? Which factors reliably make a statistically significant impact, and which don't seem to matter?
- How well do these factors explain the differences among churches' transitions?
- What happens to those results when looking at traits like church size or a church's type of governance?

The regression method is useful in allowing researchers not only to test hypotheses, but also to predict or estimate what the results might be if a church takes certain steps or has certain characteristics. After data analysis, we are left with some ideas about the best steps for churches going through a pastoral succession process—and it turns out that most recommendations are similar, regardless of the type of church or its context.

BOOSTING OUTCOMES

"How happy everyone in the transition is all comes down to relationships."

— Ron Allen, founder and former senior pastor, now apostolic missioner, of Heartland Parish, Fort Wayne, IN

Segmentation is a way of grouping people according to things they have in common. *Outcome* segmentation, then, groups people according to how their leadership transition turned out (in their self-assessment). In other words, if you put all the people who say they had an overwhelmingly positive outcome in a room together, what other things would they have in common? To find out, Barna grouped

Introduction ———— 13

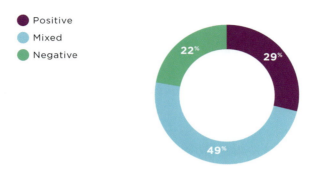

OUTCOMES AMONG CHURCHGOERS WHO HAVE EXPERIENCED A TRANSITION

- Positive
- Mixed
- Negative

churchgoers into three groups, based on a combination of questions in the survey that assessed the ultimate transition outcome: those who report a *positive* outcome (29% of all churchgoers), those who report a *negative* outcome (22%) and those whose transition outcome was *mixed* (49%). Throughout this report, we look closely at outcomes and specific factors, and share relevant insights from practitioners and pastors who have walked through succession.

Putting the Research to Work: Field Guides

Context is important for making decisions, especially those informed by data like that contained in this report. Because we want our research to help leaders turn insights into action, we have included three "Field Guides" at the end of each section (*Before*, *During* and *After the Transition*). The goal is to help you and your team take the information and start thinking about what it means for your unique context.

The report and the Field Guides can be used in any order, according to what stage of transition you and your team are in. You don't have to read from front to back, cover to cover; feel free to jump around based on your needs and interests.

The Field Guides contain four parts:

- **Team Assessment**
  This section allows you and your team to do a bit of self-assessment. We define "team" broadly to include pastors, elders, board members or other decision makers and leaders within the church.
- **Reflection Questions**
  This is an opportunity to think through the data in light of your own context.
- **Activities & Actions**
  These are some ideas for next steps or ways in which you can put the research to use in your situation.
- **Focus on the Players**
  Here you will find things that are important for the four key players in a transition: churchgoers, church staff, incoming pastor and outgoing pastor.

The Field Guides are intended to be just that: a guide that helps you in the field. Guides cannot tell you exactly what to do, but they can be a useful tool as you and your team work toward and through transitions, both now and in the future.

Whether you're in the before, during or after of a pastoral change, you can make wise decisions and strategic course corrections toward a better outcome. Let's get going!

RESEARCHERS INTERVIEWED:

- **1,517 practicing, self-identified Christians** (18 years and older) whose church had undergone a leadership transition within the past five to seven years

- **249 incoming senior pastors** who had come to their current church within the past five to seven years

- **70 outgoing senior pastors** who had left a church within the past five to seven years

- **129 church staff members** (other than the senior leader) whose church had undergone a leadership transition within the past five to seven years

Introduction   15

Be Prepared for Anything

What effect does advanced planning have on transitions?

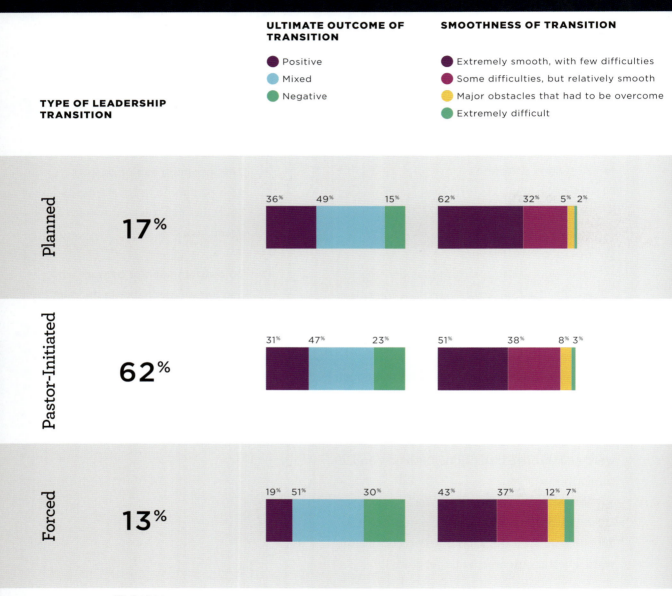

ULTIMATE OUTCOME OF TRANSITION
- Positive
- Mixed
- Negative

SMOOTHNESS OF TRANSITION
- Extremely smooth, with few difficulties
- Some difficulties, but relatively smooth
- Major obstacles that had to be overcome
- Extremely difficult

TYPE OF LEADERSHIP TRANSITION

Planned — 17%
- 36% / 49% / 15%
- 62% / 32% / 5% / 2%

Pastor-Initiated — 62%
- 31% / 47% / 23%
- 51% / 38% / 8% / 3%

Forced — 13%
- 19% / 51% / 30%
- 43% / 37% / 12% / 7%

8% don't know

While the majority of church transitions occur because a pastor initiates their departure, planning ahead for an inevitable transition makes a big difference in congregants' experiences. Barna analyzed three types of transitions: pastor-initiated, planned and forced. Transitions that are forced because of a crisis are, of course, the most difficult, but even unplanned transitions that happen for benign reasons can cause a crisis for congregants and for incoming pastors. Putting a plan in place (and acting on that plan) leads to the most positive outcomes in church transitions.

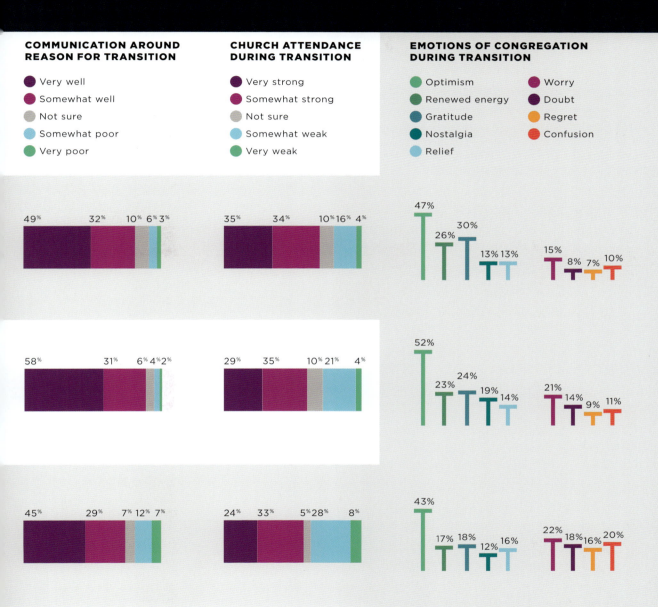

① Before the Transition

Let's start before the transition gets going. Why? Because planning ahead, as we will see, can smooth the succession process for everyone involved. Emotions often run hot during a season of change, and the more decisions made beforehand, outside the heat of the moment, the better.

Barna analysts grouped pastoral successions into three major types based on the circumstances leading up to the leadership change:

- *Planned transitions* which, as you might guess, are planned in advance of the change
- *Pastor-initiated transitions*, set into motion by a decision from the outgoing pastor
- *Forced transitions*, commenced by unexpected circumstances such as illness, death or crisis

TYPE OF LEADERSHIP TRANSITION

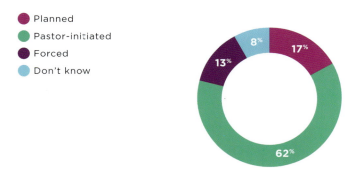

- Planned
- Pastor-initiated
- Forced
- Don't know

Researchers also looked at three *directions* of pastoral transition:

- Pastors who *step back* from the senior pastor role and move into a co-pastor or associate pastor role
- Pastors who *withdraw* from the senior pastor role into lay leadership, such as eldership or teaching, or regular membership in the congregation (a majority of the time, the impetus for moving in this direction is a pastor's retirement)
- Pastors who *depart* the congregation entirely

DIRECTION OF LEADERSHIP TRANSITION

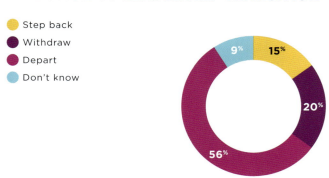

- Step back
- Withdraw
- Depart
- Don't know

Across the board, departing entirely is the most common transitional direction, but it's more common when the transition is unplanned. When a transition is planned in advance, more than half of outgoing pastors stick around, whether they step back to continue on staff or withdraw to a lay role.

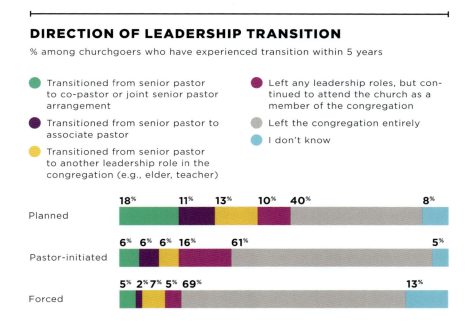

Why is this important? Because planned transitions are more likely to lead to positive outcomes once all is said and done. In general, churches where the pastor departs entirely—most common in unplanned transitions—have more tumultuous outcomes.

As you might expect, pastors who depart entirely are most likely to move on to pastor another church (34%). More prominent in the news but not as common in everyday life is the pastor who totally leaves ministry. Occasionally this is a move into a secular professional role, but often such departures are associated with personal crisis.

BENEFITS OF STEPPING BACK

"Transitioning out of the senior pastoral role freed our founding pastor for new ministry. We've worked out language and a position that frees him up to start new congregations and new missions that are still connected to our church, without having to be bogged down with day-to-day pastoral concerns. He can still be a part of everything we're doing, but have a clearer playing field, using more of his energy and time."

—Dave Frincke, senior pastor of Heartland Parish, Fort Wayne, IN

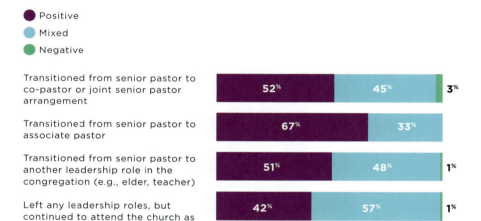

These are some of the most difficult and heartbreaking situations for a church, where members often feel hurt or betrayed *and* the church loses its credibility in the community.

Taken together, these data drive home one of the big takeaways from this research: *If you can, plan.*

Plan for Change

Again: Planning a leadership succession in advance is more likely than average to end in positive outcomes, and less likely to see negative results.

OUTCOMES OF PLANNED TRANSITIONS

- Positive
- Mixed
- Negative

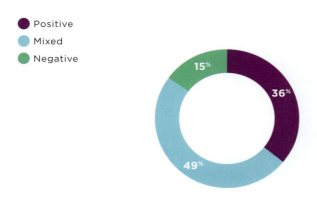

Leadership teams that plan ahead—as in, long before a transition is initiated—can shorten the overall time of a transition (once the process is kicked off), which appears to be a factor in positive outcomes. Asked about the length of their church's transition (from succession plan to completed transition) about seven in 10 church staff members report that, with advanced planning, the process was completed within a year (73%); including one-third who says transition was concluded in three months or less (34%). Conversely, transitions with no plan tend to be lengthier. In the absence of a plan, half of church staff say the transition was accomplished in under a year (53%), while one in three reports the process taking longer than one year (35%).

Involving a "multitude of counselors" in the planning process can also positively affect a pastoral transition—and, in good news, most church transitions involve multiple inputs. Most churchgoers report their transition involved teams of people, whether on a local level—such as church elders / board of directors (25%) or church members (32%)—or assembled from the leadership of a denomination (23%) or an outside church consultancy (9%). As a general rule, the higher the degree of congregants' involvement, the more positive they feel about the final outcome. Eight out of 10 churchgoers with positive outcomes agree that "the congregation had a high degree of input in the succession process" (81%), compared to six in 10 with mixed (61%) and half of those with negative outcomes (53%).

TAKE THE RIGHT AMOUNT OF TIME

"Taking time to do things right was vital, but patience was *hard*. This transition was urgent—we were in financial distress and in danger of losing our building. Our instinct after our last pastor left was to put together a search committee immediately. But our interim pastor focused us, slowing us down to the point where we could step back and assess what was vital. We took time to talk, to build relationship, reconciliation and repentance that could create congregational engagement. It was radically different, and communicated serious connection to the congregation, as if we were saying, 'Folks, you can really contribute.'"
—Church elder at Intown Community Church, Atlanta, GA

Half of incoming pastors say there was no plan before the previous pastor began to transition out (51%). In addition, one-third of incoming pastors reports that a lack of planning created extreme difficulty (12%) or major obstacles (21%) to achieving a smooth and successful transition. Even so, it does *not* appear that their predecessor's lack of planning has inspired them to do things differently. A majority of incoming pastors—who will, sometime in the future, be outgoing pastors—do not consider developing future leaders a high personal priority.

CURRENT SENIOR LEADERS ON THE IMPORTANCE OF DEVELOPING A PIPELINE OF FUTURE MINISTRY LEADERS

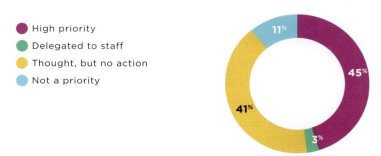

- High priority
- Delegated to staff
- Thought, but no action
- Not a priority

45% / 3% / 41% / 11%

Mentoring Tomorrow's Pastors

As pastors of today's churches age, the need to mentor younger leaders who can lead into the future is becoming ever more acute. According to Barna tracking data published in *The State of Pastors* (2017), the average age of pastors increased by 10 years between 1992 and 2017 (from 44 to 54). The generational spread also shifted during that time. While one in three pastors in 1992 was under 40, by 2017 the proportion had shrunk to one in seven. Meanwhile, the percentage of those over 65 increased more than three times; today, there are more pastors over 65 than under 40.

PASTOR AGE BRACKETS: 1992 VS. 2017

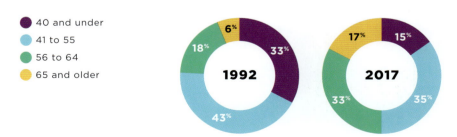

- 40 and under
- 41 to 55
- 56 to 64
- 65 and older

1992: 33% / 43% / 18% / 6%
2017: 15% / 35% / 33% / 17%

n=1,033 U.S. Protestant pastors 1992; *n*=5,067 U.S. Protestant pastors 2011–2016.

Before the Transition

Two out of three current pastors believe identifying suitable candidates is becoming more difficult (69%). About one-quarter agrees strongly that "it's harder to find mature young Christians who want to be pastors" (24%), and a larger contingent agrees somewhat (45%).

While only 18 percent strongly agree that "a lot of young leaders seem to think other kinds of work are more important than vocational ministry," more than half agree somewhat (52%).

Developing suitable young candidates for vocational ministry requires a concerted effort on the part of current pastors and churchgoers, and roughly one in five pastors strongly agrees their church "puts a significant priority on training and developing the next generation of church leaders" (22%). Almost half agree somewhat (47%).

How are they developing future leaders? Nearly three in 10 say they hired young staff and / or elected young members to leadership roles (28%), or offered training classes, camps or conferences (27%). One in six reports mentoring a young potential leader (19%), one in nine offered internships or "shadow" roles (11%) and one in 10 led small groups on discipleship and leadership (10%). Slightly rarer actions include giving encouragement and guidance to those who are considering leadership (9%) and putting resources into the youth ministry (7%).

However church leaders put it into action, identifying and training future leaders must be one aspect of preparing for eventual succession.

When Success Means More Than Succession

A Q&A with Bruce Terrell

Redeemer Presbyterian Church, founded by pastor and bestselling author Tim Keller, is one of the most influential Protestant churches in America. More than seven years ago, when Keller expressed his desire to eventually step down as senior pastor, he and his staff began preparing the church for his transition away from Redeemer and into a full-time role at the nonprofit organization City to City.

As executive director of Redeemer for the past 11 years, Bruce Terrell has overseen that transition. He reflects here on the process of moving from one church under a well-known leader to a family of three churches serving New York City.

Q. *What was the process that led to Redeemer becoming a family of three churches?*

A. Seven or eight years ago, Tim expressed that he didn't want to be the senior pastor by 2020, when he will be 70. Our mantra has always been that we're not building a great church; we're building a great city. Knowing that, we asked, "What will that mean for Redeemer in a post-Tim Keller era?"

Instead of the pressure of trying to find another Tim Keller, we felt our best strategy was to raise up new leaders, new voices and new churches for the good of the city at large, not only our congregation. Our goal was to move evangelicals in New York City from 5 to 15 percent of the population. We believe that proportion will create a tipping point for gospel renewal in the city. With that goal in mind, we decided for the time being to remain one church with Tim as the senior pastor, and transition from a multi-worship site church to a multi-congregational church.

We went from four services to eight in rapid succession. That led to us hiring lead pastors for each of those congregations. Starting about five years ago, those in the pews were hearing Tim about a third of the time, and primarily hearing from the lead pastors of their own congregations.

In addition to selecting those leaders, we moved much of the ministry we had been doing centrally to the individual congregations, including small group ministry, children's ministry and youth ministry. Our eventual goal was to create three churches, not just three congregations. Those churches, with their own governing bodies, are still part of a family of churches and ministries, which we call the Redeemer Network or Redeemer Family, but they're autonomous and independent.

Q. How did you create buy-in from the congregation throughout the transition?

A. We had to keep in mind the larger picture of succession. It didn't seem right to rush the transition and say five years ago, "We're going to identify three senior pastors, create three churches and then you're on your own. Tim is out of here."

We knew we needed a long ramp for this change, as well as proof-of-concept to show it was going to work. In many ways, it was a grand experiment to create those three congregations. We didn't know if people were going to say, "I'm just here for Tim, so therefore I'm going to find another church" or "I'll figure out which service Tim is preaching at and go there." We had some people do that, but it was a small minority.

We worked hard to communicate our 10-year vision of creating three congregations that would eventually become three churches, and we explained that our goal was for those churches to generate one new site each over the following 10 years.

Q. What advice would you have for churches undergoing a leadership succession?

A. I would strongly encourage them not to forget the spouse of the person who is leaving. Kathy Keller is the co-founder of Redeemer, and she and Tim have a remarkable partnership and marriage. They are very different, but Tim leans on Kathy a great deal, and Kathy was in significant leadership early on and really set the tone for the church.

It has been, and continues to be, very important for us to be considerate of Kathy's feelings in this process. The reality is that while the Kellers knew this needed to happen, it's still difficult. They're having to let go.

Q. Do you feel that forming the Redeemer Family of churches has been successful?

A. I would say overall it has been really successful, which is amazing when you consider we couldn't find a model of another multi-site church that created multiple churches. That meant we were building the plane as we flew it.

We did wonder if many people might leave the church, but that has not happened. In fact, I think people are even more engaged. While they love Tim and his preaching, and appreciate all his leadership has helped to create, they know Redeemer is not going to fall apart when he leaves.

People have responded very positively to their new leaders. They love their preaching and their leadership, and are glad their pastors are accessible in ways Tim hasn't been able to be. Also, now that we don't have just one or two leaders at the top, these individual churches can focus like never before on their own neighborhoods.

It's going to be fascinating to see whether we can continue to partner and collaborate as a family of churches and ministries when there is no central head. That's the next chapter of Redeemer, and we hope it will remain successful. ●

Forcing the Issue

Pastors, staff members and churchgoers involved in a forced leadership transition have a unique set of challenges and opportunities. These transitions are not initiated according to an existing plan, but because of sudden difficult circumstances such as scandal or trauma. The good news is that, while churches going through forced successions are more likely to encounter hurdles, their congregants often emerge on the other side with a positive outlook on the future.

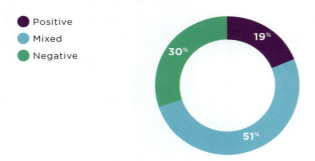

OUTCOMES OF FORCED TRANSITIONS

- Positive — 19%
- Mixed — 51%
- Negative — 30%

Not surprisingly, forced transitions are more likely than other circumstances to be fraught with issues. One in five congregants in a forced transition says there were major obstacles that had to be overcome or that the transition was "extremely difficult" (19% vs. 7% for planned and 11% for pastor-initiated transitions).

However, most congregants in forced transition churches perceive the succession as having a net-positive impact on their churches. Within a year since the transition began, congregants are much more likely to view the succession as having a positive impact on ministry priorities / styles (56% positive vs. 18% negative), staff retention (43% vs. 21%) and financial stability (39% vs. 21%). The only area where congregants have mixed feelings is weekly attendance (41% vs. 33%).

Positive perceptions among congregants are lower in forced transitions than in other types of succession. For example, forced-transition churchgoers are less likely to report seeing a positive impact on financial stability (39% vs. 57% for planned and 48% for pastor-initiated transitions) and weekly attendance (41% vs. 61% and 50%).

Asked what emotions they primarily experienced after the succession, half of forced-transition congregants report feeling optimism (50%). Further, one-third (34%) primarily experienced relief, while three in 10 report gratefulness (31%) and renewed energy (29%). These emotions closely reflect the feelings of congregants who went through other types of succession, although forced-transition congregants are more likely to experience relief (34% vs. 23% for planned transitions) and regret (10% vs. 5% for both planned and pastor-initiated transitions).

While the initial shock of a forced transition may cause uncertainty, completing the process reduces negative emotions among congregants and increases positive sentiments (see graph).

Communication is one of the strongest drivers of a successful succession and, overall, forced-transition churchgoers believe their

CHURCHGOERS' EMOTIONS DURING AND AFTER TRANSITION

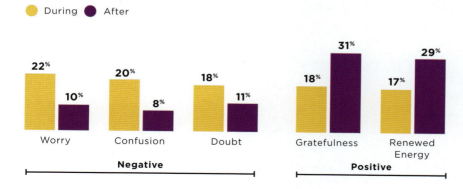

church leadership was effective in communicating the succession process. Indeed, three-quarters say the reason for the transition was communicated at least somewhat well (74%). Moreover, seven in 10 feel the same about how leadership communicated the requirements for a replacement (70%), the process for finding a replacement (69%) and the timeline of the transition (69%).

However, it's in the area of communication that leaders in forced transitions have the largest gap to close with their counterparts from planned- or pastor-initiated-transition churches. This gap in communication effectiveness likely contributes to fewer positive outcomes. Specifically, forced-transition churchgoers are less likely to say their church leaders effectively communicated the timeline of transition (69% vs. 80% for planned and 83% for pastor-initiated transitions) and the process for finding a replacement (69% vs. 81% and 83%).

A HEALING PROCESS

"It wasn't just about a leadership transition, it was about healing from a church crisis. By the time the previous pastor had left, people felt excluded and had seen their church get more and more unhealthy. There was a sense of helplessness. That turned into a positive by having so many people get involved in the transition process—even though it took a while to overcome the skepticism. Besides engaging so many people with meaningful work, they suddenly felt like they could contribute to helping make this better. That turned our two-year period of not having a pastor into a period of growth. We were busy doing meaningful things, not just busywork, but the soft relational rebuilding, working together again."

—Church elder at Intown Community Church, Atlanta, GA

While they're more likely to cause problems than other types of succession, forced transitions can have an overall positive impact on church congregants. It may not be the ideal type of succession, but the findings suggest that if managed properly and gracefully, forced transitions can result in healthy outcomes for a congregation.

Avoid (but Prepare for) the Nightmare Scenario
A Q&A with Boz Tchividjian

Basyle "Boz" Tchividjian, the third-eldest grandchild of Billy Graham, is a former prosecutor personally responsible for prosecuting hundreds of cases of child sexual abuse. He's also the founder and executive director of GRACE, or Godly Response to Abuse in the Christian Environment, an organization that educates and equips faith communities to respond well to sexual abuse disclosures, while also providing practical guidance on how to protect children and serve survivors. Their work includes conducting independent investigations into allegations of abuse by pastors and church leaders.

> **Q.** There is nothing easy about a transition involving crime or abuse. How can churches proactively plan to avoid such crises?

A. Don't idolize leaders. When one person, or a few people, become the primary focal point of the church, there's danger. Just as one example: If abuse happens, there's a strong pull to believe a certain narrative, oftentimes spun by that pastor, that *they* are the victim. The congregation loves and admires their pastor, perhaps has sat under their teaching for years, so they are usually willing to buy that.

Another problem is this: Astute abusers surround themselves with other leaders who can't lead, only enable. When problems arise, these people—who were supposed to be making the difficult decisions—simply can't. Oftentimes they'll actually turn to the accused for guidance.

The question churches need to ask is this: The longer the pastor leads the church, is Jesus or the pastor getting more prominent? If the pastor is only getting bigger, that's a dangerous trajectory.

Part of the solution is coming up with a leadership structure that minimizes one person's ability to have so much control, and limits them from placing others in leadership positions around them. If we truly understand the gospel we preach, and grasp the depths of human sinfulness, we'll realize pastors aren't immune to temptation. Those in positions of leadership are *more* susceptible than the average member of the congregation because they have more opportunities to exploit their authority.

Every church needs to make conscious, informed and intentional decisions about these issues, and lay out a polity structure that limits the authority and influence of the senior pastor.

Q. In an involuntary pastoral succession, who should churches include in the decision-making process?

A. While existing church leaders should play a vital role because they understand the church's dynamics, [there's] a lack of objectivity that can interfere with the ability to make difficult decisions. There's great value in having a diverse team and bringing in outsiders. Ideally, a team would be made up of about 40 percent congregational members, 20 percent people in church leadership and 40 percent outsiders.

One type of outsider I encourage churches to have is a retired pastor who has been trained in church transitions, or has personally experienced them. There are also pastors who've spent years as interim pastors, and perhaps one can come in during the transition period.

Q. But you're stressing the importance of being prepared.

A. Yes! It's a bad idea to wait for a crisis to decide what you'll do in a crisis. Churches need to come up with a plan that addresses both voluntary and involuntary transitions. Each must be handled differently.

In a recent investigation GRACE completed, the pastor couldn't return to ministry. Thankfully, he asked the congregation to accept and embrace the process, and that made a huge difference to the outcome. If he had not bought in, or told the congregation, "I'm being unfairly terminated; I'm the victim," it's entirely possible the church would have split.

Q. How should leaders communicate with their congregation when they are going through a crisis that forces a pastoral succession?

A. Transparency is critical. Whether they are conscious of it or not, leaders often have a low view of their congregations.

I tell leaders to intentionally look at their proposed communication first through the lens of a victim, then through the eyes of a congregation member who doesn't have all the information. It's amazing how many leaders draft communication about a serious situation and never consider how others will perceive it. Bring in some trusted members and have them read it to give their insights. This demonstrates humility. It shows that leaders know their job is to serve and love their church.

Yes, there are situations when leaders can't communicate all the details. But most members, if they sense their leaders are being straightforward and transparent with what they *can* share, will be okay with that. There's credibility and a sense of trust.

Q. *In light of the #MeToo and #ChurchToo movements, how can churches lead the way in speaking up for victims?*

A. We must deal with the past. *Every* church needs to examine its past, even if that requires getting outside assistance. Leaders should be willing to say, "If we have not addressed something properly, now is the time."

While it's going to look different for each church, this may call for a season of lament about how historically the Church has profoundly failed to protect the wounded and vulnerable, and instead protected those in power. This sense of sorrow and longing for justice must become the very DNA of our churches. It can't just be something we check off a list. This involves being humble and teachable.

Sadly, a lot of pastors and church leaders know very little about issues of abuse. They're not taught about them in seminaries, and so their knowledge comes from a particular worldview or personal experience. A sermon by a pastor who thinks they know everything about this issue, but really doesn't, can be traumatizing. Before they preach about it, pastors must take time to learn and listen to survivors—not in a patronizing way, but sincerely, knowing they have something to teach us.

I always tell pastors that when the church is handling allegations of abuse, not only is the victim listening and watching but other victims, some of whom they'll never know, are also watching and listening. Leaders must ask, "Is our response creating an environment where victims feel safe and empowered to step forward, or is it pushing them back into the shadows?"

Because if the Church is not the safest place for vulnerable and wounded people, something is wrong. ●

Field Guide ①: Before the Transition

Transitions can make everyone nervous. This field guide is focused on helping you and your team think through your specific context and begin to plan for inevitable change. The four sections below overlap with one another to help you think through preparing for transitions in different ways. This is best used in groups, or as an individual in preparation for sharing with the whole leadership team.

The ultimate goal of Field Guide 1 is to start your team thinking and planning for the future of the church and of pastoral leadership.

Team Assessment

Part 1 provides a general introduction to many of the themes of this report and discusses preliminary ideas concerning a transition. Indicate where your team is in light of what you read in this section. Consider doing this exercise individually, then compare your assessments in discussion.

	WEAK				**STRONG**
Communication within your team	1	2	3	4	5
Communication with your congregation	1	2	3	4	5
Unity of mission & purpose within your team	1	2	3	4	5
Unity of relationship within your team	1	2	3	4	5
Developed and written out transition plan	1	2	3	4	5

Reflection Questions

- After reading this section, what are the findings or themes (good or bad) that stick out to you? How do these connect with your own unique situation and context?
- Most pastors have not thought about, taken action toward or prioritized transition planning. How often is this a topic of conversation among the wider leadership team? What are the concerns, fears, plans and goals for these conversations? How can you make this a normal piece of the leadership culture?
- The importance of good communication is a key theme that emerges from the data. How good are the communication structures and patterns of your church? When it comes to transitions, have you discussed how to communicate information and to what groups should be involved at different points in time?

Activities & Action

Mapping it Out

It's time to put it on paper. What is the transition plan? It doesn't matter if you're in the middle of a transition or a transition is still five-plus years away; starting now to map it out will help your team navigate the process. Include as much detail as you can: timeline goals, communication patterns, new roles and responsibilities, involvement and input at different levels. As much as possible, have open discussion and make prayerful decisions before things get stressful and urgent.

The Emergency Plan

Some transitions are unforeseen. Talk through how you would handle an unforeseen or emergency pastoral transition. Actually write out a plan of who will fill leadership gaps and who will lead what aspects of the transition. Who will your team turn to for outside help? Make those contacts now. The emergency plan can be reviewed annually or every two years by a leadership team.

Field Guide 1

Focus on the Players

Churchgoers

Communication is key! Even in the early stages it's important to communicate clearly and often with church members. Transitions can be times of uncertainty and confusion. Communication is a key tool to help care for people during this time.

Church Staff

Transitions can be difficult for ministry leaders as well as parishioners. Communication within the team is important. As you work toward a plan, include staff members in the process. This will help shore up unity, particularly with regard to mission, purpose and relationships.

Incoming Pastor

At this point you may have no idea who the incoming pastor will be, especially if you're considering someone from outside the existing leadership. Start praying for and planning for the new pastor now. Plan for resources and relationships this person will need as they transition into your community.

Outgoing Pastor

As the current pastor transitions out of leadership or out of the community, they need care. Consider appointing a person or people to care for them and their family (don't forget the spouse!) during this time. This could be someone either within the church or outside, but should be someone who is willing to walk through this process with them to help them grow through the process.

② During the Transition

Barna's findings among congregants, church staff members, incoming pastors and outgoing pastors highlight some interesting differences in perceptions of a pastoral succession. For example, a departing senior pastor on their way out may question the wisdom of a church's leadership team, while incoming pastors and congregations tend to hope for and see the best.

Some aspects of church life, such as the teaching and a sense of unity, are likely to remain strong through the transition. Other aspects, such as financial stability and staff engagement, may weaken somewhat during the process.

Keep in mind, these perspectives are not real-time records but *reflections on experience* after the succession is complete. Regardless of how exact these judgments may be, they are valuable for understanding the paradigms and feelings of each group going through a transition so that transition leaders can plan and respond accordingly.

During the Transition   39

Let's Keep Talking
What should you communicate during transitions?

It's clear that communication is a strong factor in the experience during and success of a transition

50% OF CONGREGANTS STRONGLY AGREE THEIR CHURCH COMMUNICATED CLEARLY ON A PLAN AND PROCESS FOR SUCCESSION

My church communicated very well on…

Overall experience during transition
- Smooth
- Conflicted
- Difficult

Outcome after transition
- Positive
- Mixed
- Negative

THE REASON FOR THE TRANSITION
- 65%
- 38%
- 31%

- 74%
- 46%
- 32%

THE TIMELINE OF THE TRANSITION
- 57%
- 26%
- 17%

- 70%
- 34%
- 18%

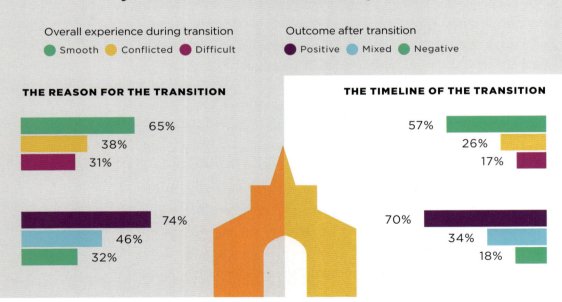

Unfortunately, communication with and to congregants is often neglected during transitions

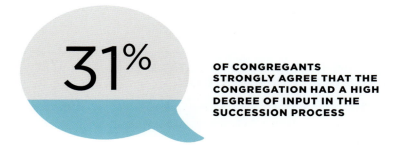

31% OF CONGREGANTS STRONGLY AGREE THAT THE CONGREGATION HAD A HIGH DEGREE OF INPUT IN THE SUCCESSION PROCESS

My church communicated very well on…

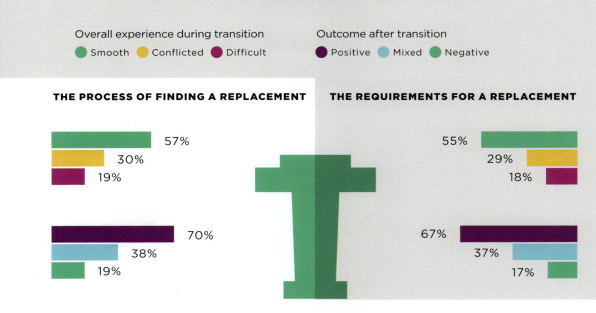

Overall experience during transition: Smooth, Conflicted, Difficult
Outcome after transition: Positive, Mixed, Negative

THE PROCESS OF FINDING A REPLACEMENT
- 57%
- 30%
- 19%
- 70%
- 38%
- 19%

THE REQUIREMENTS FOR A REPLACEMENT
- 55%
- 29%
- 18%
- 67%
- 37%
- 17%

n=1,517 Congregation / Churchgoers; n=129 Church Staff; n=259 Incoming pastors; n=70 Outgoing pastors
Fielding Dates: Church Staff & Pastor Study: March 16, 2017 – April 27, 2017; Fielding Dates: Congregation (Vendor: Nielsen): March 17, 2017 – April 4, 2017.

Teaching & Ministry Style

About one-third of respondents describes the teaching and ministry style during the leadership transition as very strong (31% churchgoers, 33% church staff, 34% incoming pastors). Incoming pastors feel most assured of this. Outgoing pastors—perhaps concerned with the legacy of their own teaching approach—are somewhat less confident in how the ministry style was maintained throughout the succession process; just one-quarter gives it a strong review.

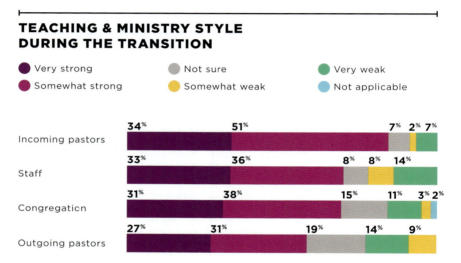

Church Finances

Roughly one-quarter of the various participants in a transition believes the church's finances were very strong through this season. And when adding those who consider it at least *somewhat* strong, about two-thirds of church staff (67%), incoming pastors (67%) and outgoing pastors (65%) had a good feeling about finances during succession. The percentage of churchgoers who are unsure is understandably greater (24%), given that they are less likely to know behind-the-scenes details like a church's financial condition.

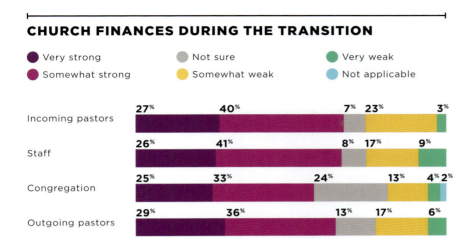

Church Attendance

Church staff (63%) and congregants (63%) align in saying that church attendance was at least somewhat strong through their church's leadership transition. Few incoming pastors say attendance was weak (18%)—in fact, three-quarters lean toward the strong side. Meanwhile, outgoing pastors are least positive in their assessment of church attendance. The gap between the perceptions of incoming and outgoing pastors is likely tied to personal emotions and expectations, and the

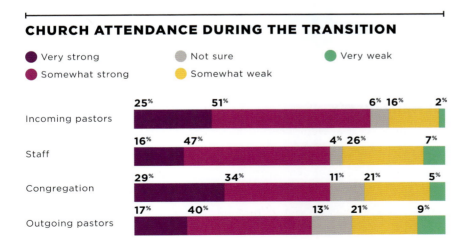

mid-range report of staff and congregants is perhaps a more reliable indicator of church health.

Staff Engagement

As the two groups with a front-row seat to a succession from beginning to end, only staff members and outgoing pastors were asked to report on the level of staff involvement in the succession process. Less than half of church staff (45%) believe they played a key part in their church's leadership transition, with an equal proportion (45%) saying staff engagement was somewhat or very weak. Outgoing pastors, on the other hand, are more likely to believe staff engagement was strong through the leadership transition (54%)—one example of outgoing pastors' seeming tendency to overestimate (or overlook) the strength of their network.

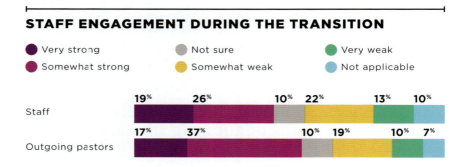

CLARITY & VULNERABILITY

"Watch your communication and deal with expectations and assumptions. Get clear on stuff. Never assume anything. Remember, this is about relational integrity and trust."

—Ron Allen, founder and former senior pastor, now apostolic missioner of Heartland Parish, Fort Wayne, IN

Unity

Although a leadership transition seems like it may stir up infighting or rumors, church members actually tend to band together. Most congregants (70%) say church unity was at least somewhat strong through a succession. A majority of other respondent groups agrees (71% incoming pastors, 68% staff, 61% outgoing pastors). Staff members, however, sometimes detect strife in the community; three in 10 (29%) rate congregational unity as very or somewhat weak.

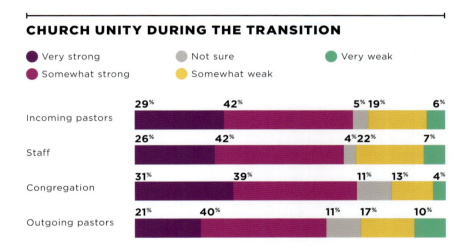

CHURCH UNITY DURING THE TRANSITION

These data are strong indicators that priorities matter. Focusing on the right priorities during a transition can make a significant difference to the outcomes of a church's pastoral succession.

Get Focused
(but *Not* on Finances)

Churches sometimes face a financial crisis at the same time they are facing a leadership transition. That's because financial troubles tend to go hand in hand with other troubles, whether in churches or elsewhere. Money is close to the human heart and is hard to extricate from relationships.

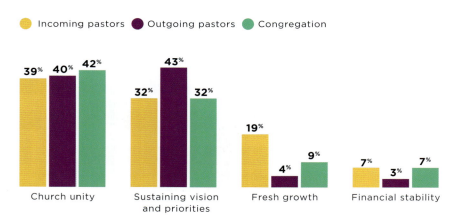

PERCEPTION OF HIGHEST PRIORITY DURING TRANSITION

● Incoming pastors ● Outgoing pastors ● Congregation

Church unity: 39%, 40%, 42%
Sustaining vision and priorities: 32%, 43%, 32%
Fresh growth: 19%, 4%, 9%
Financial stability: 7%, 3%, 7%

How should church leaders set priorities when they have not one but two crises on their hands? A good negotiating coach will tell trainees to keep asking *why* until they get to the bottom of a question. In response to *Why do we want to get the church documents in order?* "To comply with the law," is quite a good enough answer. But in response to *Why do we want to increase congregational giving?* there could be many viable answers. *We want to pay our senior pastor more. We want to engage in more mercy ministries. We want a new parking lot.*

To these answers, church leaders need to ask *why* a few more times.

46   Leadership Transitions

Out of leaders' assumptions about why their church needs something (whether or not they've explored those assumptions) come priorities, goals and even the tone of the campaign to meet a challenge.

A perception of church unity and consistent, two-way communication are more significant in determining positive outcome than a church's priorities, yet priorities *do* have a significant role to play in how well a transition goes and feels to those who experience it. Churches that focus on the big picture—vision and / or church unity—tend to have better transitions than those that focus on growth or finances.

OUTCOMES, BY CHURCHGOERS' PERCEPTIONS OF THE CHURCH'S HIGHEST PRIORITY DURING TRANSITION

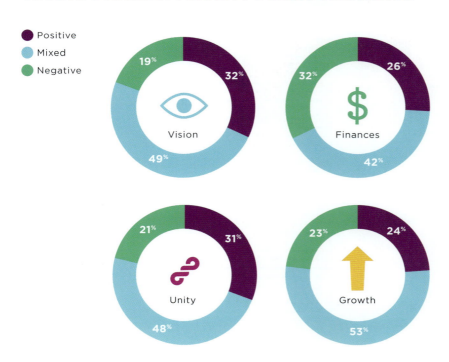

The Downsides of a Financial Focus

How can a responsible church *not* focus on financial issues when they have a financial problem? Two answers: Focusing on finances does not fix a financial problem during a leadership transition. And overall, a focus on finances is more likely to be associated with an objectively troubled transition than is a focus on other priorities.

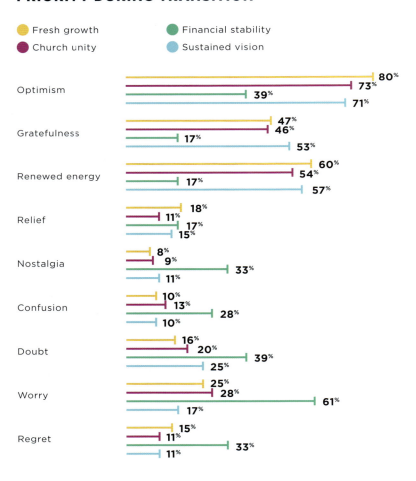

INCOMING PASTORS' EMOTIONS, BY THEIR PERCEPTION OF THE CHURCH'S HIGHEST PRIORITY DURING TRANSITION

- Fresh growth
- Church unity
- Financial stability
- Sustained vision

Emotion	Fresh growth	Church unity	Financial stability	Sustained vision
Optimism	80%	73%	39%	71%
Gratefulness	47%	46%	17%	53%
Renewed energy	60%	54%	17%	57%
Relief	18%	11%	17%	15%
Nostalgia	8%	9%	33%	11%
Confusion	10%	13%	28%	10%
Doubt	16%	20%	39%	25%
Worry	25%	28%	61%	17%
Regret	15%	11%	33%	11%

Leadership Transitions

Transitions focused on finances see worse relationships between the congregation and church leadership during the transition; just 55 percent are strong, compared to about three-quarters among churches with other goals. Likewise, transitions focused on finances and growth provoke more negative emotions during the transition. Incoming pastors whose church leadership focused on finances are much less likely to feel optimism, renewed energy or gratefulness and more likely to experience worry, regret, confusion and even nostalgia—likely for the church they left behind. Where the church prioritizes sustained vision, church unity or fresh growth (as opposed to financial stability or another goal), the congregations' emotions also tend to be more positive.

In sum, new senior pastors and congregants feel more miserable on several dimensions when their transition leaders focus on finances. With no objective gains and clear subjective strains, church leaders should consider a primary focus on finances during a leadership succession to be suboptimal.

The Upsides of a Unity Focus

If communication is king, unity is queen. Churches in all transition types benefit when there is unity between people in different roles during the process. Relationships are strong and unity is high among and between congregants, incoming pastors, staff members and elder boards. More than half of all the groups surveyed say that these relationships are strong or very strong. Meanwhile, churches with low unity tend to have other big problems, such as a lack of planning, that predictably lead to worse outcomes.

The relationships most likely to be ranked very strong by church staff are between the incoming pastor and the board of elders or directors (43%) and the incoming pastor and the church staff (40%). This indicates that staff are generally supportive of and endorse the new pastor rather than viewing him or her with skepticism.

During the Transition   49

ASSESSING THE RELATIONSHIP
BOARD OF ELDERS / DIRECTORS & INCOMING PASTOR

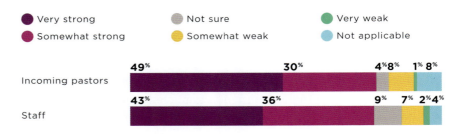

INCOMING PASTOR & CHURCH STAFF

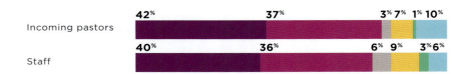

The picture for the other groups is more varied across people in different roles and is less rosy—though still positive overall. Church staff members are consistently less positive about church relationships during a leadership transition.

There is a notable difference between staff and outgoing pastors in how weak they perceive the relationship between the outgoing pastor and the board, with 42 percent of staff saying the relationship was weak or very weak and half that proportion of outgoing pastors saying so (20%). (See chart on p. 51.)

Why is the difference in perception so big? And why is there observable friction between the outgoing pastor and the board such that two out of five staff members see it? It appears that the relationship with the outgoing pastor can be hard to maintain during a transition. If strength in that relationship is a goal, then extra effort is required;

miscommunications and frustrations and hurt feelings can be very hard to overcome. Board members and staff need to recognize that outgoing pastors (even in a planned transition) are likely to be sensitive to change, nostalgic about leaving, concerned about their legacy, wanting to preserve what they built, and so on. Even when board members and staff feel like everything is going to be okay, outgoing pastors are wrestling with a lot of their own emotions.

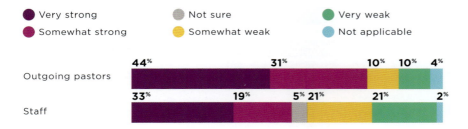

ASSESSING THE RELATIONSHIP
BOARD OF ELDERS / DIRECTORS & OUTGOING PASTOR

More than one-quarter of church staff members perceive weakness in congregational unity (29%) and in the relationship between church leadership and the congregation (27%). Churchgoers, however, are less likely to say there are problems. (It's also possible that congregants with strong feelings approach church staff and pastors, while those who are more or less content are silent.)

Most churchgoers feel close to their leadership through a transition. When members of congregations speak for themselves, about three-quarters express satisfaction with their relationship with the leadership by saying that it was very strong (35%) or strong (38%) through the transition. Likewise, most churchgoers say congregational unity is strong through a leadership transition (71%).

ASSESSING THE RELATIONSHIP
CONGREGATION & CHURCH LEADERSHIP

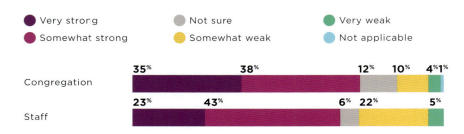

UNITY WITHIN THE CONGREGATION

A Case Study in Priorities

Even "unity," though, can be unhealthy—if it is the wrong kind of unity.

Elders from Intown Community Church in Atlanta, GA have a good deal of hindsight on this issue of developing toxic loyalty. Several years ago, their second senior pastor in two years stepped down. At the same time, they were experiencing radical losses of attendees and church leaders. The church went from 700 to 300 members. There were financial problems, big enough that one elder thought the church would lose their building because banks weren't willing to refinance. Their first attempt to repair relational damage in the church and to establish a senior pastor didn't go well.

The elders describe giving the congregation updates on the situation but not giving them a role in offering feedback or in addressing the problems themselves. One elder remembers a "growing sense of us versus them" accompanied by disconnection from the congregation.

"And then the staff also got in a foxhole, and the divisions were sharper." Since then, the elders at the church admit to a "failure to shepherd," an "inclination to circle the wagons rather than reach out" and "pursuing peace at all costs"—all common reactions by teams under stress.

Sadly, this is not an uncommon scenario. Leadership teams often pull back in emergencies, becoming more like-minded and more disconnected from those they are supposed to lead.

Group unity goes wrong when there is no dissent in a group. This may be because an authority figure is assumed to be correct in all his or her judgments—engendering a sort of "yes man" culture. This can lead to a "Team of Unrivals, in which internal diversity and dissent [are] squelched as disloyal," as Cass Sunstein wrote in *Going to Extremes: How Like Minds Unite and Divide.*

CONFLICT RESOLUTION

"The uncomfortable conversations do happen. But if you've been putting equity into relationship and building trust, you can make a choice to be vulnerable and transparent with each other. It works. Of course you're going to have problems. But like in any relationship, it's an issue of communication and then conflict resolution."

— Ron Allen, founder and former senior pastor, now apostolic missioner, of Heartland Parish, Fort Wayne, IN

Group unity goes wrong when information is limited. This may be because an elder board has neglected to listen to church staff and congregants, as in the case of Intown Community Church. It may also be because members of a board have failed to speak up when they differ from what they see as the majority.[3] Everyone loses when church leaders only hear one version of events or one strategy for leadership succession.

Group unity goes wrong when people's opinions become labels of identity, as in "Oh, he's hard-headed" or "She's one of the complainers."

During the Transition

Once people equate group membership with types of opinions, they tend to stop listening to each other.

Group unity goes wrong when misinformation and rumors have not been dealt with properly and openly.

How can boards of elders or directors and congregations avoid these pitfalls of unity?

First, "it turns out that humility and curiosity help to ensure better decisions, in large part because they increase the pool of information," writes Sunstein. Intown Community Church found that when they started listening to their congregation, the knotted problems started to loosen. They have recovered to health and have a senior pastor in place, and the elders attribute this to acknowledging their own failures and starting over with candor, honesty, transparency and vulnerability.

Second, leaders must be vigilant in seeking out information and opinions that do not confirm the majority's information and opinions. And, counter to human nature, when they encounter conflicting information and a wider range of opinions, they must treat the messengers (and opinion-holders) well and take that new information as seriously as previously known information.

Third, church leaders should be suspicious of unanimous decisions; they are actually less likely to be good ones. Church leadership should seek out and respect multiple options during a transition, and should suspect they have failed in this if they produce unanimous decisions. If they do notice many unanimous decisions, they should consider bringing in a third party to moderate.

It is important to note that disagreement is not the same as a strained relationship. Take John Gottman's research on marriage that shows "69% of problems in a relationship are unsolvable"[4] but that fighting can improve a marriage if you "fight well."[5] Unity of the best sort forms around teamwork and even team generosity.[6] In other words, teamwork doesn't just survive disagreement; it thrives with constructive disagreement.

Intown Community Church demonstrates the constructive role that healthy deliberation and communication can have in building church unity. After their difficult start, they made a concerted effort to address the problems through listening to the congregation and re-constructing a vision, calling it Project Nehemiah. They "didn't put together an immediate search committee. Instead, we took the time to assess, talk, build relationships and work on reconciliation (starting with the group of elders)." They brought in an experienced interim pastor who addressed misinformation and gossip. Despite their financial struggles, they prioritized creating "vision through congregational engagement, and then starting the search." It took time to rebuild trust in the church, but the church actually started healing before the arrival of its new senior pastor. Humility, they say, was the key.

And now? They are planning for their own successors.

Leading Differently
A Q&A with Mandy Smith

Originally from Australia, Mandy Smith is lead pastor of University Christian Church, a campus and neighborhood congregation in Cincinnati, OH. She is a regular contributor to *Christianity Today* and Missio Alliance, and is the author of *The Vulnerable Pastor: How Human Limitations Empower Our Ministry*. She is also the director of Missio Alliance's SheLeads summit and creator of The Collect, a citywide trash-to-art project. Mandy and her husband, Jamie, a New Testament professor at Cincinnati Christian University, live with their family in a little house where the teapot is always warm.

Q. Tell us about your pastoral transition. What kind of church did you take, and what kind of leader did you succeed?

A. By the time I transitioned into the senior pastor role in our congregation, I'd been associate pastor for four years, and had co-led for 18 months. It had become apparent that the lead pastor (who'd led the church for 16 years) was feeling called to justice work. He is an apostolic, courageous, justice-hearted, generous, visionary, creative, collaborative leader. He needed the space to pursue that calling.

Q. What about the process was a challenge?

A. In general the transition was quite gentle. But the change came after the pressure of "dueling callings" had been building a bit. Some of the ways the senior pastor had felt called to do justice work (such as writing and speaking at national events) had been making some people feel like he was less in touch with their local needs. That's understandable—but it's a conflict around a good issue: gospel calling. If I'm honest, at first I was resentful of how his other work was affecting the church and me. But at the same time I loved the work he was doing and was really proud of him. I felt torn.

Q. How did you respond?

A. I wrestled for months. What was the healthiest way to broach this conversation? I wanted to encourage him to pursue the things God was calling him to. He had been responsible for our congregation for so long, it hadn't crossed his mind that it was *okay* for him to feel called to something else. As I encouraged him toward that, we decided the best path forward would be for him to transition to a part-time role, and for us to co-lead together. We had thought it would be a long-term situation, but after 18 months he stepped down, and I became lead pastor.

I had no idea as I encouraged him to pursue the things God was laying on his heart, that it would not only help him step into his calling but help me step into mine. While it was difficult at times, it was quite beautiful how God walked us both through that transition and we are still great friends. I still call him for insight on leadership here.

Q. Looking back, what factors led to a successful transition?

A. Our friendship helped us navigate the transition well. Sure, we had hard conversations, but we were able to hope for the best in each other's motives and actions. Believing the best about the other person does wonders! I don't think I'd change anything. It was a surprisingly smooth transition, considering he'd been lead pastor for 19 years by the time he stepped down.

Q. What have you learned about taking over a church when your personality or demographic differs from the previous pastor?

A. A gradual transition and overlap time is ideal! It was helpful that I'd already worked as associate pastor for 4 years, then co-led for 18 months before becoming the lead pastor. We went through a process (which we are just wrapping up, six years later) of gradual changes. We didn't change the general vision (I'd been on staff before because I already valued the vision). Just changes to the specifics of how that vision is resourced and lived out.

But there could have been tremendous danger to the transition from our personal differences. I'm an introverted Australian woman who's an artist. He is an extroverted American male who is a mathematics whiz. It helped that he is an active champion for women in ministry (not just theoretical but purposeful and proactive).

Q&A with Mandy Smith

Before I came on staff, he had already walked the church through the process of welcoming women to the eldership and they'd had female pastors (campus minister, children's pastor) preach on occasion. It was the first time they'd had a female lead pastor but he walked the congregation through those conversations. When it came to personality differences, it helped that people already knew and trusted me and so knew I wasn't going to lead in the same way.

If I could go back in time and tell myself anything at the beginning of the process, it would be, "In every way you feel you're different from the previous pastor, don't be concerned that people will see it as negative."

Those differences can be strengths.

Q. *Any advice for leaders undergoing their own transition?*

A. The emotional and spiritual health of the pastors involved will be key as they have to lead the congregation through this transition even as they're navigating their own transition. It was very helpful for me to have spiritual direction once I became lead pastor. I felt my differences and needed encouragement to be myself. A role like that has a way of shaping *you*, and not always in positive ways. I had to learn to be myself in order to bring my personal pastoral strengths and gifting into play. ●

The Dos & Don'ts of Communicating During a Leadership Transition

By Samuel Ogles

Samuel Ogles is a writer, speaker, spiritual director and Enneagram teacher, and was formerly an editor at *Christianity Today* overseeing ChurchSalary and Church Law & Tax's digital presence. Based on this expertise, Barna asked him to report on communication best practices. Sam engages culture and spirituality, empowering others with deeper insights and a vision for change. You can learn more through his podcast, newsletter or website SamuelOgles.com.

Communication is just one factor in ensuring positive outcomes for a pastoral succession—but, as we've seen, it's an important one. It may also be one of the most potentially fraught areas to navigate, touching on practical and human elements as well as personnel and legal ones.

The data indicate that *clarity* of communication is key. Clear communication helps; unclear communication really hurts. To dig deeper, I interviewed William Vanderbloemen. He is the founder and leader of Vanderbloemen Search Group, an executive search firm that specializes in serving churches. He wrote *Next: Pastoral Succession That Works* with writer and church researcher Warren Bird. When it comes to pastoral transitions, "Overall, the church doesn't do a very good job with this," he says. "And it's never because people have bad intentions."

Instead, poor outbound communication around pastoral transitions tends to be the result of two things: ignorance of best practices and fear of making mistakes. To combat both and reach healthy communication, transition leaders need to know where to start.

Where to Begin

The first step, professionals say, is to know what is required by a church's constitution, bylaws or articles of incorporation. Any such governing document "is a contract between the members and the corporation on how it should be run," says Frank Sommerville, an attorney and CPA specializing in church issues. Churches are "absolutely right" to assume they're required to follow any specified rules or procedures, he adds. If they don't, it could lead to unnecessary problems, even legal action.

Apart from processes that are spelled out, however, there's a lot of room for communication about a transition. What should church leaders say and when? Who has the right or privilege to know what? It turns out, these questions are mostly answered by the answer to another: *why?*

The "why" of a pastoral transition matters as much as any other factor, and experts make a distinction between *voluntary* transitions and *involuntary* ones (in Barna's research, "forced transitions").

Forced Transitions

"The place that the church is most likely to get it right is communication to the congregation about an involuntary pastoral transition," says Vanderbloemen. This might involve the firing of a pastor or some other salacious or serious cause for the departure. Still, a common error is "mismeasuring how much of the story to share." During a difficult time like this, notes Vanderbloemen, church leaders often make the mistake of "not sharing enough." Fear of missteps could be one reason for under-communicating. If the reason for the pastor's departure is of an illicit nature, churches may wish to avoid embarrassment, a lawsuit or merely hurting the ministry through saying too much.

While churches really can't share all of the details about an involuntary transition, *not* sharing the cause will leave church members to guess at what happened, says Vanderbloemen. "People will just make up their own story," he notes, "and it's usually worse than the truth." In fact, absent an explanation, people usually assume the reason is one of two things: sexual or financial.

If the transition *is* a worst-case-scenario that touches on something as serious as a sexual or financial failure or abuse, Sommerville notes that transition leaders need to communicate clearly with the congregation, but that communication should have a lot of guardrails in place. "You basically say that the [church] board has been informed, they know what's going on, and you leave it at that," he advises. "Otherwise, it's a personnel decision that we cannot discuss publicly because we don't want to libel or slander [the outgoing pastor]." For serious issues, it's also recommended that churches utilize the services of legal counsel and potentially a public relations firm.

When it comes to transparency in communications for forced transitions, there are levels of access to information that leaders are wise to keep in mind. "Your church board is entitled to everything, pretty much—and your personnel committee. But there's nothing that says you have to share everything with every member," Sommerville cautions. "You have to be wise about what you share and don't share. You have to be measured in what you say." When offering information to the congregation or beyond, he says, offer only the facts. "At the same time, you must not lie. You have to be 100-percent truthful, no matter what."

Voluntary Transitions
In general, voluntary transitions are certainly more enjoyable to communicate about. But there are risks here, too, as well as guiding principles that can steer the pastoral transition in a healthy, clear and positive direction. Those who advise churches on this front note that communication during voluntary transitions is just as important to get right for the sake of the ministry.

Communicating about voluntary transitions, such as a pastoral retirement or succession, typically involves four pillars that have to be considered, says Erika Cole, another attorney I spoke with who specializes in advising churches on legal issues. Those four pillars are the congregation's desire for transparency, the desire for the church to control the flow of information, the incoming pastor and the outgoing pastor. Trying to balance these four is not simple—in fact, it can be quite complex.

To start, she says, church leaders should work on a succession and communication plan *before* it's needed. "Much like estate planning on the personal side, having the plan in place before you need it is key."

Vanderbloemen, with his experience doing executive searches, absolutely agrees. "Every pastor is an 'interim pastor,'" he says. Unless a church closes its doors or gets to be around when Jesus returns, the current pastor is eventually followed by someone else. In order to honor that reality, churches should think through their eventual voluntary transition plan with the same care they would an involuntary transition.

Planning ahead of time for the near inevitability of bringing in a new pastor

The Do's and Don'ts of Communicating   61

makes all the difference. In Cole's experience advising churches, "having the plan in place addresses generally 90 percent of the issues."

So what about the other 10 percent? That's where practical tips and expert guidance can make a difference.

① Guide the Narrative

David Fletcher is a former full-time executive pastor and the founder of XPastor, an organization that coaches and equips church leaders who manage the church. His advice for making the initial transition announcement is also echoed by other experts: In a healthy way, control the narrative.

"Start it with email" or a video announcement, Fletcher says. "Get your best foot forward" by crafting the message deliberately and carefully so the first way people hear about a transition is the way you want them to hear it. "And you have to tell the truth, too," he cautions. You don't want the truth coming out in another way.

② Be Faster Than the "Competition"

When you start to share the news of a transition, "it's gotta be lightning fast,"

says Vanderbloemen. Part of the reason for this approach is to be effective in communicating and part of it is to make sure a different—likely erroneous—narrative doesn't travel faster. "You might as well give them the information you want them to have," says Fletcher. This will also help negate inaccurate narratives or assumptions.

③ Get on the Same Page

Key to this initial announcement, says Fletcher, is that it is written, approved and vetted beforehand by all necessary parties. Other experts agree, and note that united understanding and buy-in are crucial.

④ Over-Communicate

There's a tendency during transitions to keep information in a close-knit circle. But absent a legal or privacy concern, it's usually better to err on the side of over-communicating, says Fletcher. A common pitfall is to keep the search process and progress secret. Search committees can too often confuse a candidate's right to confidentiality with secrecy. "It's perfectly acceptable to say, 'We have three candidates we're looking at,'" Fletcher notes.

It's a good idea to regularly update the congregation on the process, he says, whether that's an update from the pulpit, an email or just a bulletin item. Having regular touchpoints will help the congregation feel informed, even if the update is just a prayer request for the continuing progress of the transition.

Is there a danger in communicating too much? That depends on what is meant by "too much." "Too much" as in confidential details? Absolutely. "Too much" as in frequency? "There's no danger in that," reassures Fletcher.

⑤ Have a Clear Timeline

Fletcher notes that search committees tend to do a great job of communicating in the first six months or so—but then they go silent. The result is that the congregation is left to guess or newcomers are unaware of the transition process altogether. "A church can actually survive six months" out of the loop, states Fletcher. But after that, a congregation left in the dark will start to have issues with the process.

"In the communication plans we draw up," offers Vanderbloemen, "one of the axioms that has come up is 'People will walk through a really long tunnel if they know how long the tunnel is.'" Without that knowledge, he notes, anxieties arise around how much giving will drop off, what is happening with the church's ministries, and more. "All of that gets mitigated if there's clear communication." ●

Field Guide ②: During the Transition

Transitions can make everyone nervous. This field guide is focused on helping you and your team think through your specific context and begin to plan for inevitable change. The four sections below overlap with one another to help you think through transitions in different ways. This is best used in groups, or as an individual in preparation for sharing with the whole leadership team.

The ultimate goal of Field Guide 2 is to help your team think through issues that arise during a period of transition. This can be a stressful season, and leading well through this can help people develop their trust in God and remain focused on his calling for your particular congregation.

Team Assessment

Part 2 shows there are various potential priorities a church's leadership can focus on through a transition. Try to indicate where your team is in light of what you read. Consider doing this exercise individually, then compare your assessments in discussion.

	LOW PRIORITY			HIGH PRIORITY	
Church unity	1	2	3	4	5
Sustaining vision and priorities	1	2	3	4	5
Fresh growth	1	2	3	4	5
Financial stability	1	2	3	4	5

Reflection Questions

- Four factors can combine to make a toxic cocktail during periods of transitions: poor communication, lack of unity, lack of planning and a focus on finances. How have these four factors impacted or made obstacles for your team? How can you recalibrate to overcome these obstacles?

- Differences can be difficult to navigate during a transition; *listening well* is important to build unity and communicate clearly. In what ways is your team listening to one another, to the outgoing pastor, to the congregation? What is making listening difficult?

- Internal transitions have different dynamics then external ones. If you are conducting an internal transition, in what ways are you transitioning to new, homegrown leaders? How long will leaders overlap and what are you looking to accomplish during this period?

Activities & Action

Building & Maintaining Unity

Unity is key in times of transition, but unity does not mean agreeing on everything or loyalty to a particular leader. After your team has read "A Case Study in Priorities," have an open and honest discussion about unity in your team and among parishioners. Evaluate how well your team develops unity *while* allowing for different voices to disagree. What will you do and say differently?

Caring for Staff

Staff members can feel less positive during a period of transition because they see things many in the congregation don't. On top of that, they are often overlooked for special care during periods of transition. No matter where you are in the transition, develop a plan for the following staff-related issues: (1) Staff unity with incoming pastor and leadership board / team; (2) Communication of the transition process, which includes listening to their concerns, ideas and insights; (3) Pastoral care and spiritual direction for staff during this transition.

Focus on the Players

Churchgoers

Communication is key (again)! Clear, honest and frequent communication is important, even if it is difficult. Leaders tend to under-communicate, which can lead to uncertainty and church members developing their own narratives. Communication is a way to shape the narrative and help members navigate transitions well.

Church Staff

Staff members can see transitions as particularly difficult. Make sure they are continually involved in the process and have a voice during the transition. As with church members, clear and constant communication can help staff know their role and significance during periods of transition.

Incoming Pastor

This is a season with a lot of positives for the incoming pastor. Consider how this time can be used to build new relational unity with the new pastor and the leadership team. Provide plenty of space for the new pastor to ask questions without seeing them as challenging or critiquing. Be open and honest with them as they learn more about the church and assume responsibility.

Outgoing Pastor

Transitions can be very difficult for the outgoing pastor, as they are concerned with their legacy and a congregation they have cared for and led. Think through ways to keep them involved in the transition process and consider having someone (either within or from outside the church) serve as a mentor and guide for them during the transition.

③ After the Transition

Reflecting on the first year following a pastoral succession, varied perspectives surface among the four groups Barna surveyed. Staff members are split on how a leadership transition has impacted their church. Incoming pastors and their congregations perceive a very positive result, while outgoing pastors assume a more negative impact (though, granted, they might no longer be in a position to accurately assess the church's health). Staff members and churchgoers, however—the largest and thus most statistically robust samples in the study—tend to occupy the middle and are largely content with the overall experience. Whatever their reasons, that's good news! Separate from the more personal appraisals provided by incoming and outgoing pastors, there is reason to believe that most pastoral successions are ultimately of benefit to a church.

The outcomes metric we've relied on throughout this report is based in part on churchgoers' assessments of four areas impacted by the transition: ministry priorities and style, the church's finances, weekly attendance and retention of church staff. Let's look at each of these and at how staff members and pastors compare with churchgoers' perspectives.

Shifting Emotions

What emotions did you experience during the transition?

	Worry	Regret	Doubt	Confusion	Nostalgia
CONGREGATION	20%	9%	13%	12%	16%
OUTGOING PASTORS	29%	17%	20%	16%	33%
INCOMING PASTORS	26%	13%	23%	13%	11%
CHURCH STAFF	26%	12%	22%	27%	9%

No matter how much you plan, pray or prepare, successions are going to evoke a range of emotions for everyone involved. Like most changes in life, they include both something to mourn and something to look forward to. The prevailing emotions, though—for everyone from outgoing pastors, incoming pastors, staff and the congregation—are positive ones. Outgoing pastors, probably naturally, feel negative emotions at higher levels than others going through the transition.

Relief	Gratefulness	Renewed Energy	Optimism	
13%	23%	22%	48%	**Congregants** may be less negatively impacted by transitions than you might expect. Harness their optimism to spur new visions for the future.
30%	46%	33%	50%	**Outgoing pastors** may need more emotional support, encouragement and celebration as they transition out.
14%	47%	53%	71%	**Incoming pastors** can bring plenty of new energy and vision—but will need to pay attention to the mixed emotions staff and congregants may be feeling.
18%	35%	36%	60%	**Church staff** are the most likely to face confusion during times of transition. Clear communication about their roles and the new expectations will help.

n=70 outgoing senior pastors, 259 incoming senior pastors, 129 church staff who experienced church transition, 1,517 practicing Christians who experienced church transition.

Ministry Priorities & Style

Three out of five congregants and church staff members feel that, within the first year, pastoral succession had an overall positive affect on the priorities and style of their church's ministry. A significant percentage of congregants detects no change in this area—a continuity which might be seen either as a win or a loss, depending on the goals of the leadership transition. One-quarter of staff feels the first year had some kind of negative effect on ministry style, which is in sharp contrast to incoming pastors, who tend (as one might expect) to be bullish on their ministry impact.

SHIFTING FOCUS

"We were very internally focused for many years. Part of our change has been to be more outwardly open and find better balance."

—Church elder at Intown Community Church, Atlanta, GA

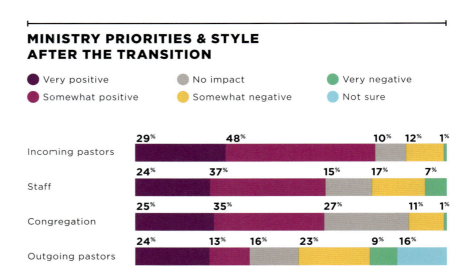

MINISTRY PRIORITIES & STYLE AFTER THE TRANSITION

- Very positive
- Somewhat positive
- No impact
- Somewhat negative
- Very negative
- Not sure

	Very positive	Somewhat positive	No impact	Somewhat negative	Very negative	Not sure
Incoming pastors	29%	48%	10%	12%	1%	
Staff	24%	37%	15%	17%	7%	
Congregation	25%	35%	27%	11%	1%	
Outgoing pastors	24%	13%	16%	23%	9%	16%

Church Finances

When discussing money, incoming pastors are once again the most optimistic, with 60 percent saying that the church's financial stability has improved since the leadership transition. Outgoing pastors give the least glowing report, and congregants fall somewhere in the middle—differences that could simply indicate a lack of awareness. These groups may not be "in the know" on the state of church finances after a pastoral succession, and so resort to their instincts: for congregants, to believe the best, and for outgoing pastors, to express some pessimism.

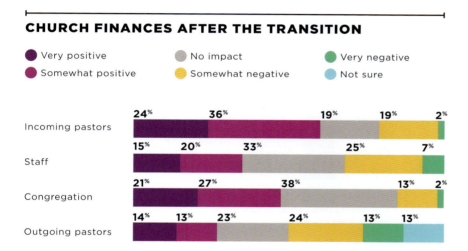

Church Attendance

The point on which the groups most struggle to agree is church attendance in the year following a leadership transition. Negative perceptions are strong among church staff, almost half of whom (45%) say there has been a negative impact on weekly attendance. The sunniest view comes from incoming pastors, suggesting there is a significant lack of consensus or communication on what is presumably a recorded (and thus difficult to quibble about) measure of success. Or, as the staff members surveyed tend to be from larger-than average churches,

After the Transition   71

it's possible that this 27-point gap is a result of the different church profiles represented by each group.

Outgoing pastors are particularly down on the state of attendance; nearly half believe there was a negative result. Those actually filling the pews—the congregants themselves—mostly perceive an uptick in numbers (50% positive), if they notice a change at all (27% no impact).

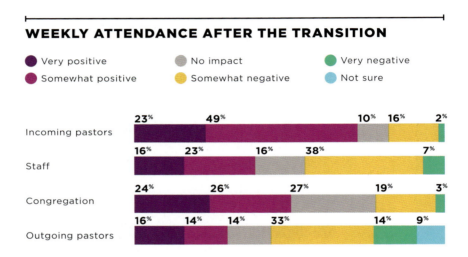

WEEKLY ATTENDANCE AFTER THE TRANSITION

Staff Retention

Although church attendance totals generate some dispute, the groups generally agree that staff numbers remained healthy in the year following a leadership transition. Staff (38%) and incoming pastors (45%)—perhaps those with the most current information on this count—usually say there has been no impact. In fact, many say this across each set of participants, though outgoing pastors are somewhat divided on whether ministry teams stayed intact. Congregants also give a fairly good update on staff retention.

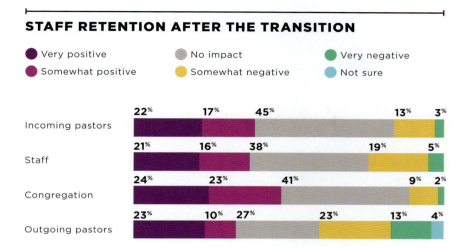

Emotions

This data is not part of the outcomes metric, but take heart: Both congregants and church staff experience a decrease in negative emotions and an increase in positive emotions after a leadership transition. (See the infographic on pp. 68–69.) Half in both groups are optimistic. Half of staff members report a sense of renewed energy within the year following a transition. Even so, this is a season during which a small but significant minority of staff members experience worry, doubt and confusion—something for transition leaders to keep in mind.

Relationship, Not Recipe
A Q&A with Darrell Hall

Rev. Darrell Hall is Campus Pastor of Elizabeth Baptist Church's campus in Conyers, Georgia. Rev. Hall's mission is to love all people into Christlikeness through the practice and preaching of the Word. He is married to Eboni and together they have three sons.

It's a long process to shape someone to carry on a church's identity. How long? For me it took 32 years—which is how old I am.

Leaders are key DNA carriers of the congregation. Our historic mother church influences my ministry through me—as fresh and new as my work might be. And that's a good thing. That heartbeat and mission are part of me. I may presently serve at a campus 40 miles away, but it still feels like home to people visiting from our mother church.

Q. *You serve today as a campus pastor for the same congregation you've attended since you were a kid. How has that lifetime of service to one church shaped your leadership and ministry?*

A. Our campus just celebrated its five-year anniversary, on the same Sunday our mother church celebrated its ninetieth. Believers for generations before us were faithful. They sacrificed and gave. We're part of that. We may be the youngest baby of the bunch, but we're part of the same family. It's my responsibility to appreciate and advance that history.

Q. *What did your church leaders do well in preparing you throughout your life in the congregation?*

A. They let me serve! I first started volunteering in our congregation when I was five. Including the younger generation is a vital place to start. Younger people are capable of so much—and it prepares them for future leadership as well as present service.

I've served in probably 15 different volunteer capacities over the years. Shoulder-to-shoulder learning—listening, leading, collaborating—is what most shaped me for my present role. There is a positive culture of training and equipping people here. In general, it's a relational process rather than a recipe.

Q. *You're a young leader on the "upward" transition path. That can go to a young leader's head. What are you learning about navigating that?*

A. When a transition is upon us, we have an opportunity to check ourselves, whether we're the ones exiting the office or entering it. Losing or gaining it does not change who a person is or their intrinsic value. Your influence may have changed. Your importance has not.

At the cusp of a transition, we have extra energy to examine ourselves. There is excitement, remembrance and intentionality for the next season. I can mostly speak from the perspective of transitioning "up" into positions of more responsibility. Over the past 16 years, that's been my journey, starting out as a Bible study leader for our choir, then transitioning into our adult ministry, as a preaching assistant to our senior pastor, then youth pastor, and now serving as a campus pastor. At each level, who I am in Christ is important—it's the place I serve from.

I think danger comes in when a person—especially if they are young—"leapfrogs" levels of ministry. Growth is usually gradual. It's a grace to go up by the stairs rather than the elevator. Each step begins a season of disequilibrium, where you have to regain your bearings before resettling into your fundamentals in Christ.

Q. *What else should we remember about transitions?*

A. Times of transition have a way of humanizing spiritual leaders.

When a leader is at the peak of their tenure, there can be this dynamic, like Joshua, who God made "large in the eyes of the children of Israel." That "big" quality of a leader can fade in transition, because they are leaving the position they needed it for. They often don't exude the same confidence. They often aren't larger than life anymore.

But the transition humanizes them. Moses led his people through the Red Sea, then ended his life in an anticlimactic moment, alone on a mountain, not getting to go into the Promised Land. We think, *wait, what just happened?* He just *dies*. But the ministry keeps moving.

Do we give our leaders space to be human? Especially in transition? Often not. Bitterness can come up, anger. Natural human emotions that need to be processed. That's part of what it feels like to be a *person*. A person with feelings. Our pastoral robes or clerical collars are not bulletproof.

Q&A with Darrell Hall ⸺⸺ 75

Leaders hurt. Many pastors learn to serve in spite of that. But when you transition out of a role, it catches up to you. There needs to be space to process the whole range of shortcomings that might have happened in that role. *Who do I need to forgive? Who might need to forgive me? Am I carrying pain? How is the Lord using this to make me more like Christ?*

When I moved out of my youth pastor role I felt some guilt. I felt I could have done more with the position. I felt frustration—there had been so much more I'd had in my heart to accomplish as a youth pastor. Moving on was right, but I still felt that. I had to acknowledge my mixed feelings to bring emotional closure to that season and move forward to the next season.

Keeping a good name is different than having a great title. At the end of the day, no matter how I serve, I'm still Darrell Hall, on my knees before God, just like on the first day of my call. We all must learn to minister out of that settled place. ●

Going Out & Coming In: Two Different Views

Analysts wanted to compare how a leadership transition affects both incoming and outgoing pastors. Not surprisingly, the findings indicate these two groups experience succession distinctly from one another and have opposing views on how the church has progressed after the transition. Let's take a look.

Views on the Overall Process

Overall, both incoming and outgoing pastors believe the transition went smoothly. That said, outgoing pastors are less likely to say the transition went at least relatively smoothly (69% vs. 81%).

Both incoming and outgoing pastors provide positive ratings when asked to look at the strength and weakness of different relational components. For example, both rate their relationship with the board of elders or directors during the transition as strong (79% incoming pastors vs. 75% outgoing pastors), as well as the relationship between the congregation and church leadership (74% vs. 72%).

There are, however, some stark differences between the two groups. Outgoing pastors are less likely to view the following as strengths during the transition: ministry style / teaching (58% vs. 85% incoming), church attendance (57% vs. 76%) and unity in the congregation (61% vs. 71%). Overall, outgoing pastors have a less positive view on the health of the church and the shift in teaching styles.

Emotions During the Transition

Given the differences in how they view the transition, it's not surprising that incoming and outgoing pastors *feel* the experience quite differently as well. Overall, as one might expect, incoming pastors appear to have a heightened level of excitement and energy, looking forward to their new role. And while outgoing pastors are more apt to feel positive emotions than negative ones, they tend to be more reflective about the past during the transition. Indeed, incoming pastors report experiencing primarily higher levels of optimism (71% vs. 50% outgoing) and renewed energy (53% vs. 33%), while outgoing pastors are more likely to experience nostalgia (33% vs. 11% incoming). Interestingly, outgoing pastors are also more likely to experience a sense of relief during the transition (30% vs. 14%). This may be linked to the longer process that outgoing pastors face: informing the congregation, providing necessary assistance during the search process and then transitioning their duties to the next senior pastor.

While differences abound, incoming and outgoing pastors still share some key emotional experiences. (See the infographic on pp. 68–69.) Nearly half report feeling gratefulness (47% incoming vs. 46% outgoing). Both groups, however, also experience a similar level of worry (26% vs. 29%) and doubt (23% and 20%).

At the end of the day, both groups appear to believe they made the correct choice; only about one in seven experiences some sense of regret (13% incoming vs. 17% outgoing).

Differing Priorities

When asked to identify their highest priority during the succession, a plurality of both groups says maintaining church unity (39% incoming vs. 40% outgoing). However, incoming pastors are less likely to prioritize sustaining the vision and priorities (32% vs. 43%) and more likely to prioritize fresh growth (19% vs. 4%). Given that outgoing pastors are feeling nostalgia during the transition, it's possible that seeing a lower priority on sustaining the vision is unsettling. After all, these are the vision and priorities they have been championing to the congregation for years.

This difference in perceived priorities may be linked to their contrasting beliefs about who initiated succession. Incoming pastors are less likely to say it was the previous senior pastor who initiated the process (46% vs. 61% outgoing). Since incoming pastors are apt to think the decision for a change in leadership came from elsewhere in the church, it's possible that they correspondingly see sustaining the vision and priorities as less important during the succession.

Assessment of Impact

Perhaps the strongest contrast between incoming and outgoing pastors is the perceived impact the succession made on the church in the first year. As you'll recall, the majority of outgoing pastors are no longer part of the congregation. Thus, their perceptions of the church in the year after the transition may be driven more by their experience *during* the transition or by anecdote.

Incoming pastors overwhelmingly believe the succession has had a net-positive impact on their church. Indeed, the majority of pastors views the succession as having a positive impact on ministry priorities and styles (77% positive vs. 13% negative), weekly attendance (72% vs. 18%) and financial stability (60% vs. 21%).

By comparison, outgoing pastors believe the succession has had a negative impact on weekly attendance (47% negative vs. 25% positive), financial stability (37% vs. 27%) and staff retention (36% vs. 27%). While the views of outgoing pastors may not be based on first-hand knowledge, they should not be ignored. Handing over leadership to another individual is inevitably tricky for outgoing pastors, but it is made even more difficult if they genuinely believe the church they shepherded is worse off now than when they were the pastor. ●

DIFFERENCES ARE OKAY

"When you become a successor, you step into an established environment of relationships, behaviors and systems, and people choose to stay or leave based on what you bring to the culture and whether or not they connect to it. It was midway through the second year that the full weight of the transition hit me: I found myself dealing with a lot of comparison between me and my successful predecessor and it triggered some unresolved rejection in me. In the midst of a really painful season of self-doubt I discovered that God's grace is always sufficient, whether you're letting go of your current position, or stepping into a new role to lead. And, on a practical level, I also learned, after the fact, to let someone filter your email for you during times of transition. Getting input from the right people will keep you healthy and help you to stay focused on the most important things."

—Terry Crist, pastor of Hillsong Phoenix, AZ

Don't Waste Your Crisis
A Q&A with Doug Sauder

Before becoming a youth pastor, Doug Sauder worked as a teacher and a coach. He joined the staff of Calvary in January 2000 and served as a family pastor and President of 4KIDS of South Florida. Doug currently serves as Lead Pastor at Calvary Chapel, joining Calvary's Board of Directors in May of 2014. Doug and his wife, Suzanne, have three sons.

Q. In many ways, you inherited a nightmare scenario for succession. What was the immediate aftermath of the former pastor's resignation?

A. Calvary Chapel is the largest church in our community, so there were significant shockwaves, internally and externally. The former pastor was a dynamic speaker with big personality, and he was a spiritual father to many. That breach in trust goes deep. There were rumors the church was going to fall apart, that it had been built on one person's celebrity and couldn't survive without it.

True, in that first month we lost about 20 percent of our congregation and of our giving. But after that, nothing catastrophic happened. We stabilized, and began to move forward.

Q. What stands out to you from the early transition?

A. How we as leaders had to process alongside our congregation. Our staff found out on a Wednesday about the former pastor's failures, which were really serious. He resigned on Thursday. We read the church his resignation on Sunday. As staff, we were only three days ahead of the congregation in our shock and grief.

After accepting his resignation, our board of directors stepped in. Their response was united and firm, but also *beautifully* prayerful. "How do we shepherd the congregation? How will we support our new lead pastor—whoever that will be—and our team?" One of our board members took a week off work and just answered phone calls. We worked together.

But we needed care, too. Some of our staff and other people had personal issues come up because of what happened. There were people from the outside who helped, particularly two counseling centers in Florida. When it came to offering help to our former senior pastor, we called experts from outside our state, and they created a plan with us.

I think of Colossians 1, which says that "in Christ, all things hold together." So many people were praying for us. We felt like Jesus was fighting for our church. There was holiness, and even a sense of romance to it because in the middle of all the grief and shock, God was working. Just one example: a church we had never heard of sent us care packages along with letters that said, "We went through this a year ago. We just want you to know you're going to make it." That was like water in a desert.

Q. Tell us about your succession process.

A. Initially, there were several high-profile leaders both within and outside the Calvary Chapel movement who told our board and staff the only way to keep a church our size going was to "hire a rock star." But none of us felt good about that—it felt like part of the problem. We needed to rebuild trust, and we wanted a more authentic church.

But in the meantime, we needed leadership. There was a core team of four teaching pastors (I was one), who'd preached when the former pastor wasn't in the pulpit. The people knew and trusted us, and we formed a crisis team with the board. However, we quickly realized we needed a captain. The board asked me to pray about serving that way, and a month later, I stepped into the lead pastor role.

There were so many ways it wasn't ideal. But I realized, *I'm picking up a baton that was dropped. It wasn't a good hand off, but I'm going to run with it, and someday, I'll hand my baton to someone else.*

Q. Did anything make the transition smoother?

A. Two things: real leadership unity and easing into the role. Early on, the board and executive team of pastors met daily to pray. The sentiment was, "We're in this together. If we stay united, we'll make it. If we become divided or political, we'll fall apart." That set the course for everything.

When things began to stabilize, the board of directors *slowly* stepped out. It was beautiful. At first, the chairman of the board was leading our meetings. Then the next meeting, I would talk a little more, and he would talk a little less. Before long I was leading. It was a gentle transition.

Q. What have you learned about taking over from a different personality?

A. To give myself permission to be myself, and not be defined by my predecessor. We are *completely* different in leadership, background and personality. When he was our pastor, the church was more focused on *his* personality and *his* message. I'm more of a team player and perfectly content to have someone else up front.

I will never be him. Humor is just one example. When he preached, you'd laugh several times every service. If I'm lucky, every *other* service I'll get a chuckle. I have had to grow here: My wife tells me, "Don't try to be funny. Just be yourself." My role is not to become what was before, it is to lead faithfully.

Q. How did you guide the congregation through the grieving process?

A. By being honest. People talk about the stages of grief when someone dies—denial, anger, bargaining, depression and acceptance. Our congregation went through

each of them. It was challenging, especially because our leadership team was grieving too. We had to lead through our own pain.

There was a lot of raw emotion. Deep feelings of betrayal. We had to process that with people. I remember one lady yelled at me between services: "You hypocrites!" A week later she called me. "I'm sorry," she said, "I'm just so angry. I don't know what to do with my anger." I told her, "It's okay. Let's pray together."

For the first month and a half, our running joke was that no leader was having a phone conversation less than an hour long. People asked *everything*, from "Did you guys know about [the former pastor's] issues? Were they covered up?" to "Is my whole spiritual experience real? Can I even trust God and other people?"

The first six months were a vortex. Then things began to settle. It was chaotic and beautiful. We called it "horribly wonderful."

Q. What would you tell a church walking through a similar situation?

A. Don't waste your crisis. Use it for God's purposes. Externally, our vision expanded. Internally, our staff culture changed. What happened could be more than a cautionary tale. It could be a catalyst.

We spent a year and a half asking our

Q&A with Doug Sauder

staff, "What kind of work culture do you want?" We brought in a consulting firm to assess the health of our church. That process highlighted two things: We wanted our leaders to demonstrate humility, and we needed to provide soul care for our staff. We didn't want a celebrity culture, or the sense that "we're the best church." We wanted to be healthy and right with God, and authentic in our relationships.

The process of succession has been very clarifying. We're a simpler church than before. I can't say I'd want to go through an experience like this again, but we've learned a lot of good things. It has been healthy and holy. ●

Caring for Pastors

One thing incoming and outgoing pastors have in common is that the process of transition can be a strain for them and their families.

The transition tends to be hectic time for incoming pastors across a number of fronts. Three-quarters are relocating for their new role (76%), and two in five of those are moving from out of state (41%). Nine out of 10 incoming pastors are married (91%), and more than half have children under the age of 18 living with them (54%). Given the need to uproot their families to a new location, it's not surprising that half of incoming pastors agree that the transition was difficult for their family (49%).

Two in five incoming pastors were at their previous church for over 10 years (40%), with one-quarter having more than 15 years in their previous role (23%). These leaders are not just leaving their former jobs behind; in many cases they are physically moving away from friends and neighbors they have cared for over a span of many years.

Amid uprooting their families and leaving behind friends, incoming pastors do not always arrive at their new churches to an environment that makes the transition process easy for them. Only one in five has a period of overlap with the previous pastor (19%) before assuming full duties. Moreover, just half agree that a clear plan for succession was in place before the transition started (51%).

MULTIGENERATIONAL LEADERSHIP

It was in both our hearts to have a multigenerational church where we didn't 'kick grandpa out of the house.' What would it look like to have a founding pastor who hands off the church but doesn't leave? The founding pastor becomes a 'grandparent,' and because we were able to navigate that in a healthy way, it put to rest natural feelings, like 'Wow, this church is radically different all of a sudden,' or, 'Where is my pastor for the last 30 years?' Well, actually, he's still here. He's still on staff. He still gets paid. He's still on the team. That made the transition smooth for our congregation."

—Dave Frincke, senior pastor of Heartland Parish, Fort Wayne, IN

On the flip side, the transition process can be a difficult time for outgoing pastors as well. A similarly high number of outgoing pastors are married (94%), though they are less likely to have children under the age of 18 living with them (21%). Despite differing family compositions, outgoing pastors are equally likely to agree the transition was difficult for their family (53% vs. 49% of incoming pastors).

Nearly half of outgoing pastors have been the senior pastor at the church they are leaving for more than 10 years (44%), with three in 10 having a tenure that spanned more than 15 years (31%). Three out of five left their congregation entirely after the succession (59%). Similar to incoming pastors, outgoing pastors are leaving more than just a job; they are adjusting to changes in relationships with friends and neighbors they have cared over for many years.

In addition to all of that, outgoing pastors also have to grapple with passing their legacy on to someone else—in many cases, to someone they do not know personally, since four out of five incoming pastors were not previously involved with the congregation (82%).

So how can transition leaders and churchgoers assist and support both incoming and outgoing pastors? In two key ways.

Family Support

Given that most incoming pastors are moving to a new location and have families, church leaders and congregants should do all they can ease the burdens that come with uprooting a family and replanting it in a new location. This might include putting together a task force of congregants with the purpose of assisting the incoming pastor's family during the move. Help could include:

- Providing the family with information about potential neighborhoods to move into and information about potential schools

- Connecting the family with real estate professionals from the congregation or community
- If the spouse is employed, surveying the congregation for contacts that work in his or her field

Many outgoing pastors are leaving to take a new role in a different church elsewhere. Likewise, church leaders and congregations could put together a task force to provide the same type of assistance for the outgoing pastor's family as they prepare to relocate to a new city. It may also be wise, depending on the circumstances that led to the transition, to provide professional counseling support to the pastor and their family.

Work Support

Perhaps the best thing church leaders can do for incoming pastors is to have a succession plan in place that overlaps with the outgoing pastor. Indeed, regression analysis shows that having the outgoing pastor stay in the church as an associate pastor or attendee is a top factor that leads to a more successful transition. At the very least, having a clear plan in place removes another item off the list for incoming pastors and can allow them to better focus on their family during the change, and learn more about the congregation during the transition.

If the outgoing pastor is retiring, consider asking them to stay on as an associate pastor or honorary pastor-at-large. The ongoing presence of the outgoing pastor not only increases the likelihood of a successful transition, but may also allay any notion that the church is worse off post-transition. Such a move also allows the outgoing pastor to maintain the relationships and support they have built up over the years and communicates the value congregants have for the outgoing pastor's legacy at the church.

After the Transition 87

Field Guide ③: After the Transition

Transitions can make everyone nervous. This field guide is focused on helping you and your team think through your specific context and begin to plan for inevitable change. The four sections below overlap with one another to help you think through transitions in different ways. This is best used in groups, or as an individual in preparation for sharing with the whole leadership team.

The ultimate goal of Field Guide 3 is to help your team think through issues that arise after transition. It's important to keep in mind that finding / hiring a new senior pastor doesn't end the transition; rather, transitions are long processes that need to be attended to even after the new pastor is officially installed.

Team Assessment

There are always unintended consequences or unforeseen impacts of a transition. Use the tool below to help identify some of these in your particular context.

Where have you seen *positive gains* for your church community since the transition?

Teaching / ministry	Mission clarity	Finances
Church unity	Staff unity	Staff development
Church attendance	Volunteerism / serving	

Where have you seen *problems* for your church community since the transition?

Teaching / ministry	Mission clarity	Finances
Church unity	Staff unity	Staff development
Church attendance	Volunteerism / serving	

Reflection Questions

- In what ways has this transition been a benefit for the mission God has called your congregation to? In what ways has it been an obstacle to your mission?
- A new senior leader can have a significant impact on the church staff who work with him or her regularly. How has the transition impacted your staff? Try to think of specific examples.
- Have you thought about a post-transition plan? What should the first year look like for the new pastor, for the staff, for church ministry? What goals have you set and how are you going to care for the congregation and staff after walking through this transition?

Activities & Action

Taking the Emotional Temperature

Often people act out of emotion more than reason, and thus it is important to understand the emotional place people occupy. Consider doing an emotional survey of your church staff and congregation six months and then 12 months after the transition. You may want to use the emotional categories listed in the infographic on pp. 68–69 of this report.

Caring for Pastors

Change is hard for everyone, but especially on pastors' families. Appoint a small group of leaders to be the "pastors to the pastor" in the year following the transition. Follow up with them and their families; look for ways to bless them unexpectedly.

Focus on the Players

Churchgoers

Many congregations express optimism and renewed energy after a transition. This can be a great tool for kingdom advancement. Try to leverage this while also recognizing that even the best transitions carry some sense of loss.

Church Staff

Staff may still have lingering negative emotions after a transition. Consider ways in which you can care for and support the church staff in learning to lead with a new lead pastor.

Incoming Pastor

Incoming pastors are often very positive about the transition. Consider how you can help them settle into their new position while giving them space and freedom to use their gifting with the staff and church.

Outgoing Pastor

Connections with the outgoing pastor will depend on a variety of factors, including if they retired, moved churches or left under negative circumstances. If possible and appropriate, consider how their work and labor can be remembered and honored within the community, and how you can support them and their family emotionally and spiritually.

Predicting Negative, Mixed & Positive Transition Outcomes

Risk Factors

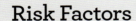 **NEGATIVE OUTCOMES** **MIXED OUTCOMES**

SOME PERCEPTIONS AND EXPERIENCES MAKE A NEGATIVE OUTCOME MORE PROBABLE . . .

Communication Breakdown
People feeling left in the dark often ends in a rougher overall transition. Those who disagree strongly that "the plan and process for the succession were clearly communicated to the congregation" are more prone to report a negative outcome than those who agree strongly with the statement.

"The relationship between church leaders and the congregation was very strong."
● 6% ● 42% ● 52%

"The relationship between church leaders and the congregation was very weak."
● 70% ● 16% ● 14%

Congregation Disintegration
People who sensed congregational unity was very weak through the transition are apt to assess outcomes as negative, while those who felt "we're all in this together"—that unity was very strong—are more likely to say the transition was positive overall.

"Unity within the church staff was very strong."
● 5% ● 41% ● 54%

"Unity within the church staff was very weak."
● 62% ● 26% ● 12%

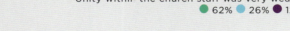

Failing Finances
Additional data points from the study suggest that making financial stability the church's top priority is not the wisest choice—but ignoring it altogether is also risky. Those who perceived the church's finances as very weak through the process are also likely to believe the outcomes were ultimately negative.

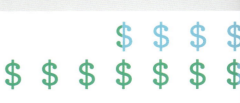

92

What factors lead to success... or success in the eyes of the congregation? The outcomes metric suggests that poor communication, disunity in the congregation and financial uncertainty correlate with a person's negative assessment of the transition. Meanwhile, responsive leaders, a unified ministry staff and the former pastor's ongoing involvement in the church are associated with more positive perceptions of the ultimate outcome.

POSITIVE OUTCOMES

Reward Multipliers

...AND A FEW MAKE A POSITIVE SUCCESSION EXPERIENCE MORE LIKELY.

"The plan and process of succession were communicated very clearly."
● 14% ● 45% ● 41%

"The plan and process of succession were not communicated clearly."
● 56% ● 35% ● 8%

Strong Ties Between Leaders & the Led
When people feel a very strong bond between themselves and those leading the church through the transition, they are much more likely to say the ultimate outcomes were positive. But those who rate the leaders-congregation relationship as very weak tend to have had a rougher time by the end of the process.

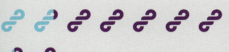

"Congregational unity was very strong."
● 5% ● 41% ● 54%

"Congregational unity was very weak."
● 63% ● 19% ● 17%

Staff on the Same Page
Harmony among the other pastors and ministry staff helps to ensure a smoother transition. Those who say unity within the church staff was very strong are more likely than those who perceived staff unity as very weak to report succession was a success.

"The church's financial stability was very strong."
● 4% ● 40% ● 56%

"The church's financial stability was very weak."
● 66% ● 24% ● 9%

n=1,517 U.S. practicing Christians 18 and older who have experienced pastoral transition within the past five years.

5 Marks of Successful Leadership Transition

By David Kinnaman, President of Barna Group

Here are five of the top factors—derived from regressions and outcome segmentation—associated with successful leadership transitions.

① Communicate Clearly, Honestly & Often

It's difficult to exaggerate the importance of this first factor. Evidence of good communication, especially between a church's leadership and congregation, is the single biggest factor in a smooth leadership transition—and the inverse is often true as well.

This trend persists regardless of the events that precipitate a transition. Even when a leader is leaving under tragic or scandalous circumstances, with all the delicate or unsavory details from which the leadership might want to shield their congregation, communication is key. Throughout this report, we see over and over that the best emotions, decisions and outcomes of a leadership transition are associated with churches that communicate well throughout the process. With this in mind, it's encouraging that most churchgoers in Barna's sample give solid scores to their leadership's communication—and those who report overall positive outcomes score their leadership even higher than average.

② Target Unity

This variable is a combination of perceptions about the relative strength or weakness of unity between the congregation and the church leadership; unity within the congregation; unity among the board of elders / governing body; and unity among other church staff / administration. A high level of church unity is associated with good communication, a smooth succession process and positive outcomes within one year after succession.

Some negative emotions consistently accompany a *lack* of unity—namely, worry, doubt and confusion. Across the board, the outcome of a transition corresponds to the emotional experience: A positive outcome goes hand in hand with positive emotions; mixed outcomes are accompanied by mixed emotions; and negative outcomes carry their share of negative feelings. Churchgoers who experience a difficult transition tend to feel worry, regret, nostalgia and confusion, and fewer positive feelings. These congregants also struggle to rebound or renew their energy post-transition, but instead see increases in regret, doubt and nostalgia, with a corresponding decrease in gratitude.

On the other hand, churchgoers and church staff members who have a sense that "we're all in this together" are much more likely to feel hopeful.

WORKING AS ONE

"There were all these different layers to the transition, but what kept us anchored was that we were united. We were committed to a common outcome. We saw the future and knew that we were better together for going the distance. Because of that vision, we didn't allow anything to divide us in the process."

—Terry Crist, pastor of Hillsong Phoenix, AZ

③ If You Can, Plan

The reason for a pastor's departure affects the experience, emotions and perceived outcomes of a transition. In short, planned departures go more smoothly, while forced or unplanned transitions are worse on multiple outcomes. And yet, pastors and staff members in this study are split on whether their church had a clear succession plan in place before their transition started. Only about half of churches, at best, appear to have a plan. And those plans are least apparent to staff.

A CLEAR PLAN WAS IN PLACE BEFORE THE TRANSITION STARTED

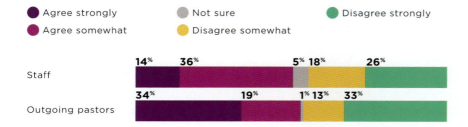

- Agree strongly
- Agree somewhat
- Not sure
- Disagree somewhat
- Disagree strongly

Staff: 14% / 36% / 5% / 18% / 26%
Outgoing pastors: 34% / 19% / 1% / 13% / 33%

5 Marks of Successful Leadership Transition   97

Congregants have the best overall experience with planned transitions and / or those where the outgoing pastor chooses to retire. Thirty-six percent of churchgoers in these circumstances ultimately report a positive outcome within a year of the transition.

It's not that other transition types are always a bad idea. Indeed, they are sometimes unavoidable—and, regardless of the precipitating circumstance, most ultimately turn out okay. As mentioned above, strong communication can cover a multitude of succession sins. But a "make-it-up-as-we-go" approach simply has less of a chance of going smoothly, and often fails to find time and intention for other steps that improve a transition, like including multiple types of input in the decision-making. If a governing body can plan ahead for a transition, the church is likely to come out ahead.

④ Aim for a Graceful Exit

Although controversial leadership transitions draw more attention, a majority of successions are prompted by a pastor's retirement or unforced move. Yet regardless of the reason a pastor transitions out of their full-time role, they undergo a dramatic life shift. The outgoing pastor is at the center of succession—in more ways than one, and not always for the best. In many cases they are experiencing some level of trauma or crisis, even as they express a sense of nostalgia (33%) or relief (30%) about leaving their post. More than half say the succession process is tough on their family (53%), and some pastors and staff members indicate weakening relationships through a succession.

However vulnerable pastors may be in this season, their next steps often correlate with the overall outcome of a succession, and Barna finds that baby steps are the ideal. When pastors exit the pulpit gradually—assuming a co-pastor or associate role, if only for a time, rather than a sudden or permanent absence from the church body—the transition seems to go better for all involved. Ideally, a pastor's period of stepping down overlaps with the stepping up of a new senior pastor, rather than an interim leader. (This scenario is obviously most likely in churches that have a succession plan in place.)

FOLLOWING THE NEW LEADER

"You have to let go. You just absolutely must. I determined I wasn't going to give Terry, my successor, any advice unless he asked me. If anybody told me they didn't like something, I deflected it and simply replied that Terry and Judith have been so supportive and honoring of us."

—Gary Kinnaman, former pastor of Hillsong Phoenix, AZ

"I think the greater burden is on the leader leaving more than the leader coming in. If you're transitioning out, you have to be secure and patient enough to see this work. You can't open your mouth any time you feel like it. You can't micromanage. You can't become that old guy who just doesn't know how to let go. The older team member *has* to be willing to relinquish your hold and not have the final say. That's just the bottom line—especially if you are going to stay at the church."

—Ron Allen, founder and former senior pastor, now apostolic missioner, of Heartland Parish, Fort Wayne, IN

⑤ Keep Asking *Why*

It's important to be aware of the motivations behind a succession process, not just the out-front decisions. Leadership teams hold different concerns for their churches during a transition, and Barna asked about potential priorities. By far the most common priority—stated by leaders and observed by their congregations—is to maintain church unity, followed by a desire to see the vision sustained. These two goals tend to coincide with positive emotions, strong communication and healthy relationships among leader teams and members.

Only a minority of respondents indicates that financial stability or fresh growth were the top priority through a transition, and that appears to be for the best: A succession focused on finances or growth is likely to take longer (a common trait of difficult transitions) and have more negative side effects, like staff turnover. Further, concern over money isn't necessarily the most effective rallying cry for incoming senior pastors, who feel more miserable and detect a weaker connection among the church's lay leaders when the focus is on finances.

A church's priority during a pastoral succession is another factor that, on its own, doesn't make or break a church and that can be mitigated by robust communication and relationships. But the intent of a pastoral succession has repercussions that are significant enough to caution teams to be very intentional and prayerful about setting—and revisiting—their long-term transition goals.

ON THE IMPACT OF VALUES

"The values of the transition worked their way positively into the congregation. It changed the way we elders relate to the regular member. But it took a boatload of self-examination individually and collectively, speaking the truth in each other's lives. It was worth it, but it was not easy."

—A church elder at Intown Community Church, Atlanta, GA

These five themes pop up again and again throughout this report. They are the essentials of pastoral succession, as revealed by the data and reflected in secondary sources.

Pastors and their ministries can't afford to put off thinking about succession. Ultimately, there is no single proven formula for ensuring it goes well; each transition is as unique as the leader and church involved. But planning early, thoroughly and openly is as important as the substance of those plans. And, more than anything, communication across teams and congregations is the heartbeat of healthy transitions.

If you are a pastor, no matter your age or tenure at your current church, it's time to think about future leadership. Who are the young adults and even teens in your congregation who are already leaders? Who among them demonstrates pastoral impulses to care for others, inspire action and speak up? Who do you see expressing a deep hunger to serve Christ? Make mentoring tomorrow's church leaders a priority of your own ministry.

Whether you are a pastor or a lay leader, start the succession conversation *now* among your fellow leaders. It may be awkward at first, especially if the senior pastor is not planning to retire any time soon, but the only way to normalize talking about an uncertain future (even a very distant future) is to get started and then keep at it until it becomes normal. Long before a change is on the immediate horizon, working through Field Guide 1 together can help your church be ready when the day comes.

More than anything, good communication across teams and congregations is the heartbeat of healthy transition. Now is the time to assess communication strengths and weaknesses, to broaden and hone inadequate skills, and to deepen relational roots so that you thrive together in every season to come.

APPENDIX

A. Additional Contributors

Ron Allen, founder and former senior pastor, now apostolic missioner, of Heartland Parish, Fort Wayne, IN

Ron Allen has been a pastor for over 54 years. He and his wife, Carolyn, have overseen the planting of over 120 churches. They planted Heartland Church in 1985 and handed it off to Dave and Bethany Frincke in 2015. They continue to serve on staff.

Terry Crist, pastor of Hillsong Phoenix, AZ

Terry Crist and his wife, Judith, are Lead Pastors of Hillsong Phoenix, which has campuses in Scottsdale, Mesa, Phoenix, Glendale, Tucson and Las Vegas. He has traveled into more than 65 nations to speak in churches, at conferences and on university campuses. Terry and Judith have three adults sons, three daughters-in-law and two grandchildren. The entire Crist family is engaged in serving and building the local church.

Dave Frincke, senior pastor of Heartland Parish, Fort Wayne, IN

Dave Frincke is a sixth-generation pastor who has a passion for music, the arts and equipping people for ministry. After helping to plant a church in Virginia, he returned to Fort Wayne, Indiana, with his wife, and came on staff at Heartland Church in 2010 to lead the worship community. He became Senior Pastor of Heartland in 2015. Dave is the co-founder and movement leader of United Adoration (UA), an international movement focused on equipping local congregations to write and sing their own worship songs. He is a priest in the Anglican Church in North America (ACNA) and lives in Fort Wayne with his wife and four children.

Gary Kinnaman, former pastor of Hillsong Phoenix, AZ

Gary Kinnaman served as Senior Pastor of Word of Grace Church (now Hillsong Phoenix) for 25 years. Under his leadership, the church grew to an average weekend attendance of more than 4,500. He now serves as a pastor-at-large, mentoring and networking church, government and marketplace leaders to serve the Phoenix area. His most recent book is *Seeing in the Dark: Getting the Facts on Depression and Finding Hope Again*. Gary and his wife, Marilyn, make their home in Gilbert, AZ, and have three adult children and nine grandchildren.

APPENDIX

B. Notes

1. William Vanderbloemen and Warren Bird, *Next: Pastoral Succession That Works* (Grand Rapids, MI: Baker Books, 2014), 9.

2. Vanderbloemen and Bird, Next, 10.

3. Cass R. Sunstein, *Going to Extremes: How Like Minds Unite and Divide* (Oxford University Press, 2019).

4. Michael Fulwiller, "Managing Conflict: Solvable vs. Perpetual Problems," The Gottman Institute, July 2, 2012. https://www.gottman.com/blog/managing-conflict-solvable-vs-perpetual-problems/ (accessed March 2019).

5. Daniel Coleman, "Want a Happy Marriage? Learn to Fight a Good Fight," *The New York Times*, February 21, 1989. https://www.nytimes.com/1989/02/21/science/want-a-happy-marriage-learn-to-fight-a-good-fight.html (accessed March 2019).

6. Anik, Lalin, Lara B. Aknin, Michael I. Norton, Elizabeth W. Dunn, and Jordi Quoidbach, "Prosocial Bonuses Increase Employee Satisfaction and Team Performance," *PLoS ONE* 8(9): e75509. doi:10.1371/journal.pone.0075509 (accessed March 2019).

Notes

APPENDIX

C. Methodology

The findings of this study are based on surveys of pastors, church staff, and churchgoing Christians.

A total of 249 incoming and 70 outgoing senior pastors completed a quantitative online survey in March and April 2017. These pastors were recruited from Barna's pastor panel (a database of pastors recruited via probability sampling on annual phone and email surveys) and are representative of U.S. Protestant churches by region, denomination and church size. All respondents were screened to include those who had been part of a senior pastoral transition in the last 5–7 years. The margin of error for incoming pastors is +/- 6.2% at the 95% confidence level and +/- 11.7% for outgoing pastors. Outgoing pastors data is primarily for comparison purposes due to small sample size.

Using the same U.S. Protestant pastor panel, Barna also asked pastors to invite church staff members who had experienced a senior pastor succession in the past 5–7 years to complete a similar online survey. A total of 129 staff members qualified and completed the survey. The margin of error for church staff members is +/- 8.6% at the 95% confidence level.

Finally, a sample of 1,517 church-going, self-identified Christians (18 years and older) were recruited from an online research panel. Respondents were screened to ensure they had experienced a senior pastor transition in the past 5–7 years and completed an online survey about their experience. At the 95-percent confidence level, the maximum sampling error on the practicing Christians survey is +/- 2.5%.

APPENDIX

Acknowledgements

Barna Group wishes to thank our partners at Brotherhood Mutual, especially Mark Robison and Mitzi Thomas.

Many thanks also to our wise and generous contributors, without whose experience and insights this report would be considerably less useful to those doing the everyday good work of the local church: Darrell Hall, Samuel Ogles, Doug Sauder, Mandy Smith, Boz Tchividjian, Bruce Terrell and the elders of Intown Community Church.

The research team for *Leadership Transitions* is Brooke Hempell, Caitlin Shuman, Traci Hochmuth, Inga Dahlstadt, Susan Mettes and Aly Hawkins. Under the editorial direction of Roxanne Stone, Aly Hawkins and Alyce Youngblood created this report with contributions from Jeremy Alexander, Charles Allers, Susan Mettes, Steve Olson and Paul Pastor. David Kinnaman and Brooke Hempell added analysis and insights. Doug Brown edited the manuscript. Roxanne Stone and Aly Hawkins developed the data visualizations, which were, along with the report, designed by Annette Allen. Brenda Usery managed production with project management assistance from Mallory Holt.

The *Leadership Transitions* team wishes to thank our Barna colleagues Amy Brands, Daniel Copeland, Bill Denzel, Aidan Dunn, Cory Maxwell-Coghlan, Pam Jacob, Savannah Kimberlin, Steve McBeth, Jess Villa and Todd White.

APPENDIX

About the Project Partners

Barna Group is a research firm dedicated to providing actionable insights on faith and culture, with a particular focus on the Christian church. In its 35-year history, Barna has conducted more than one million interviews in the course of hundreds of studies, and has become a go-to source for organizations that want to better understand a complex and changing world from a faith perspective.

Barna's clients and partners include a broad range of academic institutions, churches, nonprofits and businesses, such as Alpha, the Templeton Foundation, Fuller Seminary, the Bill and Melinda Gates Foundation, Maclellan Foundation, DreamWorks Animation, Focus Features, Habitat for Humanity, The Navigators, NBC-Universal, the ONE Campaign, Paramount Pictures, the Salvation Army, Walden Media, Sony and World Vision. The firm's studies are frequently quoted by major media outlets such as *The Economist*, BBC, CNN, *USA Today*, the *Wall Street Journal*, Fox News, Huffington Post, *The New York Times* and the *Los Angeles Times*.

www.Barna.com

Brotherhood Mutual is a national property and casualty insurance company with a heart for helping churches thrive. The company was founded in 1917 with a commitment to "Bear One Another's Burdens" and more than a century later, Paul's words to the Galatians continue to serve as a guide for its employees and independent agents. As a leader in the industry, Brotherhood Mutual provides innovative insurance coverage and risk management resources, specifically designed for ministries, to help them operate safely and effectively. The company looks toward the future, working with and anticipating the unique needs of churches, Christian schools, colleges, camps, and related ministries across the U.S. Additionally, Brotherhood Mutual provides access to payroll and tax filing services, commercial auto insurance, worker's compensation insurance, and mission travel insurance.

www.BrotherhoodMutual.com

Knowledge to Lead with Confidence

The Mercy Journey
Equipped with the findings of this introspective study, be challenged to pursue more thoughtful conversations and compassionate endeavors in a hurting world.

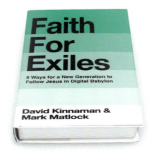

Faith for Exiles
Enter the world of resilient young adult Christians: learn how they are sustaining faith and find hope in all that God is doing among young disciples today.

Households of Faith
Discover the ways practicing Christians' core relationships engage them in a thoughtful, transformative faith—the kind that holds up to and is passed down over time.

Reviving Evangelism
A number of factors are curbing many Christians' enthusiasm for faith-sharing, including some non-Christians' suspicion of people of faith. Where does that leave evangelism?

AVAILABLE AT BARNA.COM/RESOURCES